Taxcafe.co.uk Tax Guides

How to Save Tax
2011/2012

By Carl Bayley BSc ACA

Important Legal Notices:

Taxcafe®
TAX GUIDE - "How to Save Tax 2011/2012"

Published by:
Taxcafe UK Limited
67 Milton Road
Kirkcaldy
Fife
KY1 1TL
Tel: (0044) 01592 560081
Email: team@taxcafe.co.uk

First Published, March 2002
Fourteenth Edition, April 2011

ISBN 978-1-907302-46-6

Disclaimer
Before reading or relying on the content of this Tax Guide please read carefully the disclaimer on the last page which applies. If you have any queries then please contact the publisher at team@taxcafe.co.uk.

Pay Less Tax!

...with help from Taxcafe's unique tax guides and software

All products available online at

www.taxcafe.co.uk

Other popular Taxcafe titles include:

- *How to Avoid Property Tax*
- *Tax-Free Property Investments*
- *Salary versus Dividends*
- *How to Avoid Inheritance Tax*
- *Non-Resident & Offshore Tax Planning*
- *The World's Best Tax Havens*
- *Tax Saving Tactics for Non-Doms*
- *Small Business Bookkeeping, Tax & VAT*
- *Using a Company to Save Tax*
- *Selling Your Business*
- *Using a Property Company to Save Tax*
- *Master Property Capital Gains Tax in 2 Hours*
- *The Investor's Tax Bible*
- *Property Capital Gains Tax Calculator*
- *How to Build a £4 Million Property Portfolio*
- *How to Avoid Tax on Foreign Property*

About the Author

Carl Bayley is the author of a series of plain English tax guides designed specifically for the layman. Carl's particular speciality is his ability to take the weird, complex and inexplicable world of taxation and set it out in the kind of clear, straightforward language that taxpayers themselves can understand. As he often says himself, "my job is to translate 'tax' into English".

Carl enjoys his role as a tax author, as he explains: "Writing these guides gives me the opportunity to use the skills and knowledge learned over almost twenty-five years in the tax profession for the benefit of a wider audience. The most satisfying part of my success as an author is the chance to give the average person the same standard of advice as the 'big guys' at a price which everyone can afford."

Carl takes the same approach when speaking on taxation, a role he frequently undertakes with great enthusiasm, including his highly acclaimed annual 'Budget Breakfast' for the Institute of Chartered Accountants.

In addition to being a recognised author and speaker on the subject, Carl has often spoken on taxation on radio and television, including the BBC's 'It's Your Money' programme and BBC Radio 2's Jeremy Vine Show.

Carl began his career as a Chartered Accountant in 1983 with one of the 'Big 4' accountancy firms. After qualifying as a double prize-winner, he immediately began specialising in taxation.

After honing his skills with several major international firms, Carl began the new millennium by launching his own tax and accounting practice, Bayley Miller Limited, through which he provides advice on a wide variety of taxation issues; especially property taxation and tax planning for small and medium-sized businesses.

Carl is a member of the governing Council of the Institute of Chartered Accountants in England and Wales and a former Chairman of ICAEW Scotland. He has co-organised the annual Peebles Tax Conference for the last nine years.

When he isn't working, Carl takes on the equally taxing challenges of hill walking and writing poetry and fiction. Carl lives in Scotland with his partner Isabel and has four children.

Dedication

For the Past,

Firstly, I dedicate this book to the memory of those I have loved and lost:

First of all, to my beloved mother Diana – what would you think if you could see me now? The memory of your love warms me still. Thank you for making it all possible;

To my dear grandfather, Arthur - your wise words still come back to guide me; and to my loving grandmothers, Doris and Winifred;

Between you, you left me with nothing I could spend, but everything I need.

Also to my beloved friend and companion, Dawson, who waited so patiently for me to come home every night and who left me in the middle of our last walk together. Thank you for all those happy miles; I still miss you son.

For the Present,

Above all, I must dedicate this book to the person who stands, like a shining beacon, at the centre of every part of my life: Isabel, my 'life support system', whose unflinching support has seen me through the best and the worst. Whether anyone will ever call me a 'great man' I do not know, but I do know that I have a great woman behind me.

Without her help, support and encouragement, this book, and the others I have written, could never have been.

For the Future,

Finally, I also dedicate this book to four very special young people: Michelle, Louise, James and Robert.

I am so very proud of every one of you and I can only hope that I, in turn, will also be able to leave each of you with everything that you need.

Thanks

First and foremost, I must say an enormous thank you to Isabel: for all her help researching everything from obscure points of tax legislation to popular girls' names in Asia; for reading countless drafts; for making sure I stop to eat and sleep; for putting up with me when I'm under pressure and, most of all, for keeping me company into the 'wee small hours' on many a long and otherwise lonely night. I simply cannot ever thank her enough for everything that she does for me, but I intend to spend the rest of my life trying!

Thanks to the Taxcafe team, past and present, for their help in making these books far more successful than I could ever have dreamed.

I would like to thank my old friend and mentor, Peter Rayney, for his inspiration and for showing me that tax and humour can mix.

And last, but far from least, thanks to Ann for keeping us right!

C.B., Roxburghshire, April 2011

Contents

Investment Bonds
Partnership and other Trading Losses
Film Relief
Lloyds Underwriters
Business Premises Renovation Allowances

Introduction and Warning
Pension Contributions
The Annual Allowance
Pension Input Periods
Is It Worth It?
Annual Allowance Charges
Transitional Relief
The Lifetime Allowance
Valuing Your Pension Pot
Defined Benefit Schemes
Indexing Scheme Values
Valuing Defined Benefit Schemes for the Lifetime Allowance
Tax Relief for Pension Contributions
The 'Earnings' Problem
Higher Rates of Relief
Pension Contribution Guidelines 2011/12
Wealth Warning for all Higher-Rate Taxpayers

Tax Returns
Tax Payments
The Self-Assessment 'Double Whammy'
What If Income Reduces?
Self-Assessment and PAYE
Investment Income and PAYE
New Sources of Untaxed Income
New Traders
Wealth Warning re Foreign Interest
Personal Pension Payments made directly by Employers

Gift Aid Donations
Higher Rate Taxpayers
Basic Rate Taxpayers
Starting Rate and Non-Taxpayers
Carrying Donations Back to the Previous Year

Further Benefits
Gift Aid and Pension Contributions
Gift Aid on Admissions to Museums, Etc.
European Charities

'Family Allowances'
PAYE and National Insurance
Higher Salaries for Family Members
Year-End Planning
Accelerate or Defer
Small Business Taxation Review

Corporation Tax Rates
Should Small Companies Accelerate Taxable Income?
Using Your Own Personal Allowance
Using the Basic Rate Tax Band – Dividends
Using Dividends to Avoid 'Super Tax'
Dividends Paid to Spouses, Partners & Other Family Members

Detailed Example
Reducing Payments on Account

Practical Implications
Low CO_2-Emission Cars
Alternative Fuels
Vans
Zero Emission Cars and Vans
Fuel Benefit
Multiple Tax Increases
Cars Not Available

Tax Credit Claims
Provisional Claims

Introduction

Welcome to Taxcafe's *How to Save Tax 2011/2012*, our comprehensive guide to tax planning for the 2011/12 tax year.

This publication provides an overview of most of the major tax-planning measures available to help the reader save tax in three main areas: Income Tax, Capital Gains Tax and Inheritance Tax. More detailed advice is available from our specialist tax guides, available on the Taxcafe.co.uk website.

Many of the tax planning strategies outlined in this guide require action by the end of the tax year on 5th April 2012. Some of the resulting tax savings will be immediate, other measures will bear fruit later. The common factor in most cases is the need to take action by a specific deadline, which will often be 5th April 2012.

If you decide to follow some of the advice in this guide, remember that you will need to allow time for professional advisers, banks and other institutions to process your instructions. We recommend that you take action sooner rather than later, where possible.

Remember also that each person's own situation is unique. Whilst this guide is intended to be as helpful as possible, it is no substitute for professional advice and we cannot take any responsibility for any action which readers may take, or may choose not to take, as a result of reading this guide.

The Current Tax Year

The current tax year runs from 6th April 2011 to 5th April 2012. I will generally refer to it as '2011/12'.

Chapter 1

Just How Much Tax Do We Pay?

Before we get into the tax planning, it is perhaps worth stopping to think just how much tax we are all paying.

The tax rates and allowances applying for 2011/12 are set out in Appendix A. But what do all of these various rates, reliefs, tax bands, etc. mean for the individual taxpayer?

The exact amount of tax which each individual will pay for the tax year 2011/12 depends not only on the level of your income, but also on the type of income. Each of us will have a different mix of income types, giving us all a unique tax profile.

In this chapter, however, I will look at the simplistic situation where we assume that the individual receives only one type of income.

We will start by looking at the position for taxpayers under state retirement age and then look at older taxpayers later.

Income Tax Rates

Most types of income are now subject to Income Tax at three rates: 20%, 40% and 50%. Interest and other savings income is also subject to a 'starting rate' of 10%. Different rates apply to dividends.

Where total income exceeds £100,000, the individual's personal allowance is withdrawn at the rate of £1 for every £2 of income above this threshold. This generally creates an effective marginal Income Tax rate of 60% on income between £100,000 and £114,950.

The £100,000 threshold is based on 'adjusted net income': that is taxable income less 'grossed up' gift aid and personal pension contributions. This means that these reliefs are now worth a lot more to people in this marginal tax bracket and we will return to this point in later chapters.

Employment Income

In addition to Income Tax, employment income is also subject to Class 1 National Insurance at a rate of 12% on earnings between £7,225 and £42,475 and 2% on any further earnings above £42,475.

The combination of Income Tax and National Insurance produces effective total <u>combined</u> tax rates on employment income, as follows:

First £7,225:	Nil
£7,225 to £7,475:	12%
£7,475 to £42,475:	32%
£42,475 to £100,000:	42%
£100,000 to £114,950:	62%
£114,950 to £150,000:	42%
Over £150,000:	52%

In addition to these sums, the employer must also pay secondary National Insurance at a rate of 13.8% on all payments to employees in excess of £7,075 per annum.

Whilst this further charge is paid by the employer, it naturally adds to the cost of employment. This in turn limits the level of salary which the employer is able or willing to pay. Hence, although only suffered indirectly, this further National Insurance cost is, in truth, effectively borne by employees themselves.

Taking all of this into account, we see that the total tax suffered on different levels of employment income for 2011/12 is as follows:

Income	Income Tax	Employee's NI	Total paid by Employee	Employer's NI	Total Tax Suffered
£10,000	£505	£333	£838	£404	£1,242
£20,000	£2,505	£1,533	£4,038	£1,784	£5,822
£30,000	£4,505	£2,733	£7,238	£3,164	£10,402
£40,000	£6,505	£3,933	£10,438	£4,544	£14,982
£50,000	£10,010	£4,381	£14,391	£5,924	£20,314
£100,000	£30,010	£5,381	£35,391	£12,824	£48,214
£150,000	£53,000	£6,381	£59,381	£19,724	£79,104
£200,000	£78,000	£7,381	£85,381	£26,624	£112,004

Self-Employment

The self-employed pay Income Tax at exactly the same rates as employees.

The National Insurance situation is, however, completely different.

Instead of Class 1 National Insurance at 12%, the self-employed pay Class 4 National Insurance at the lower rate of 9%.

There is no employer's secondary National Insurance but, for all self-employed taxpayers with annual earnings over the 'small earnings exception' limit of £5,315, there is also Class 2 National Insurance of £2.50 per week.

This time, the combination of Income Tax and National Insurance produces effective total <u>combined</u> tax rates on self-employment income, as follows:

First £5,315:	Nil
£5,315 to £7,225:	£130 (fixed cost)
£7,225 to £7,475:	9%
£7,475 to £42,475:	29%
£42,475 to £100,000:	42%
£100,000 to £114,950:	62%
£114,950 to £150,000:	42%
Over £150,000:	52%

Partnership trading income is also subject to exactly the same tax regime. The total tax suffered on different levels of self-employment or partnership trading income for 2011/12 is as follows:

Income	Income Tax	Class 2 NI	Class 4 NI	Total Tax Suffered
£10,000	£505	£130	£250	£885
£20,000	£2,505	£130	£1,150	£3,785
£30,000	£4,505	£130	£2,050	£6,685
£40,000	£6,505	£130	£2,950	£9,585
£50,000	£10,010	£130	£3,323	£13,463
£100,000	£30,010	£130	£4,323	£34,463
£150,000	£53,000	£130	£5,323	£58,453
£200,000	£78,000	£130	£6,323	£84,453

Landlords

If there is one great virtue which can be attributed to property rental income, it surely must be the fact that it is generally exempt from all classes of National Insurance.

Landlords receiving rental income only will pay Income Tax at the same rates as detailed above for employment or self-employment income, but have no National Insurance liabilities.

Investment Income

Investment income is also exempt from all classes of National Insurance but is subject to a slightly different Income Tax regime from earned income or property income.

For tax purposes, we must divide investment income into two categories:

- Interest and other savings income not classed as dividends
- Dividends

Interest and Other Savings Income

The 10% starting rate of Income Tax was abolished for all other types of income in 2008, but continues to apply to interest and other savings income not classed as dividends. This income is therefore currently subject to Income Tax at four rates: 10%, 20%, 40% and 50%.

It is important to note that the 10% starting rate can only apply where the taxpayer's other income (excluding dividends) is low enough to enable their interest and other savings income to fall into the starting rate band.

Hence, individuals aged under 65 on 5th April 2012 will generally only be able to benefit from the starting rate band in 2011/12 if their other income for the year (excluding dividends) is less than £10,035 in total.

Subject to this point, the effective tax rates on interest and other savings income for 2011/12 are as follows:

First £7,475:   Nil
£7,475 to £10,035:   10%
£10,035 to £42,475:   20%
£42,475 to £100,000:   40%
£100,000 to £114,950:   60%
£114,950 to £150,000:   40%
Over £150,000:   50%

Dividend Income

For all dividend income, UK or foreign, the actual Income Tax rates applying are as follows:

First £7,475:   Nil
£7,475 to £42,475:   10%
£42,475 to £150,000:   32.5%
Over £150,000:   42.5%

However, in practice, the position is considerably more complicated. For each 90 pence of dividend actually paid by a company, a tax credit of one ninth, or 10 pence, is added. This produces a 'gross' dividend of £1.

The recipient is then treated as having received a dividend of £1. When calculating their tax liability, however, the taxpayer may then deduct the 10 pence credit.

The practical upshot of all this is that when one looks at the tax payable on the actual amount of dividends received, the effective Income Tax rates on most dividends are actually 0%, 25% or 36.1%.

For dividends falling into the marginal tax bracket where the individual's personal allowance is being withdrawn, the effective Income Tax rate depends on what other income they have in the same year and ranges from 37.5% to 48.6%. For those with dividend income only, the marginal tax rate in this bracket will be 37.5%.

The 'grossing up' under the tax credit system also has another effect – it reduces the size of the tax bands by one tenth. This produces the following effective tax rates for individuals receiving dividend income only in 2011/12:

First £38,227.50:	Nil
£38,227.50 to £90,000:	25%
£90,000 to £103,455:	37.5%
£103,455 to £135,000:	25%
Over £135,000:	36.1%

Foreign Dividends

Before 2008, the one ninth tax credit described above did not apply to any dividends received from foreign companies (i.e. companies not resident in the UK).

Today, however, the tax credit also applies to all foreign dividends except where the recipient individual owns 10% or more of the share capital in the paying company and that company is resident in a 'tax haven'.

Investment Income: Summary

To summarise the position, the Income Tax suffered for 2011/12 on investment income is as follows:

Income	Income Tax Suffered On:			
	Property Income	Interest Income	Dividends	Tax Haven Dividends*
£10,000	£505	£249	£0	£253
£20,000	£2,505	£2,249	£0	£1,253
£30,000	£4,505	£4,249	£0	£2,253
£40,000	£6,505	£6,249	£443	£3,253
£50,000	£10,010	£9,754	£2,943	£5,946
£100,000	£30,010	£29,754	£16,693	£22,196
£150,000	£53,000	£52,744	£31,292	£40,875
£200,000	£78,000	£77,744	£49,347	£62,125

* - Dividends from a shareholding of 10% or more in a company resident in a 'tax haven'

The tax applying to any foreign income is also subject to any Double Tax Relief which may be available.

Pensions

Pensions received by individuals aged under 65 are taxed at the same rates as apply to property income, as shown above.

The position for older taxpayers is, however, somewhat more complex, as we shall now examine.

Older Taxpayers

All of the above rates and tables apply to male taxpayers aged 16 to 64 and female taxpayers aged between 16 and state retirement age.

Younger and older taxpayers are exempt from National Insurance.

For those reaching state retirement age (currently 65 for men and somewhere between 60 and 61 for women – see further below), the exact date on which National Insurance ceases to apply depends on the type of income:

- For employees, the exemption applies to any amounts normally due for payment on or after the date that state retirement age is reached.

- For self-employed individuals, the exemption is not applied until the tax year after the one in which they reach state retirement age. [Except for those reaching state retirement age on 6th April, who are exempt from National Insurance for the tax year beginning on that date]

Employers must continue to pay secondary National Insurance on payments to employees over state retirement age.

Individuals aged 65 or over by the end of the tax year are also entitled to a higher personal allowance. The personal allowance is increased again at the age of 75. (These age limits are not dependent on gender.)

An additional married couples allowance is also available to married couples and civil partners where at least one spouse or partner was born before 6th April 1935. For those who married before 5th December 2005, the allowance is usually claimed by the

8

husband but the couple may elect that the spouse with the higher income should claim the allowance instead.

In the case of eligible couples marrying or entering civil partnerships on or after 5th December 2005, the allowance must be claimed by the spouse or partner with the higher income.

Details of these age-related allowances are included in Appendix A.

The age-related allowances are all withdrawn at the rate of £1 for every £2 of income over a designated 'income limit'. This limit stands at £24,000 for 2011/12. The minimum married couples allowance of £2,800 is not subject to withdrawal, however, and the normal personal allowance of £7,475 is not withdrawn until income reaches £100,000.

The result of all these variations is to produce no less than nine different sets of effective tax rates for those over state retirement age and their spouses or civil partners.

However, once any individual over state retirement age receives income (other than dividends) of more than £38,220 in total, the effective tax rates on any additional income (other than dividends) are (almost) always as follows:

£38,220 to £42,475:	20%
£42,475 to £100,000:	40%
£100,000 to £114,950:	60%
£114,950 to £150,000:	40%
Over £150,000:	50%

(The 'almost' above refers to a few cases where income other than interest, other savings income and dividends is less than £12,650.)

Space does not permit me to consider every possible permutation of the tax rates applying to income under £38,220 received by individuals over state retirement age, but it is worth examining a few of the most common scenarios.

Our first scenario covers a woman over state retirement age on 6th April 2011 (see below) but who will be aged under 65 on 5th April 2012 and who is not eligible to claim the married couples allowance. The effective tax rates applying to her employment, self-employment, pension or property income for 2011/12 are as follows:

First £7,475:	Nil
£7,475 to £42,475:	20%
Over £42,475	As above

In other words, a woman in this position simply pays Income Tax at the normal rates but escapes National Insurance.

Our second scenario covers an individual over state retirement age on 6th April 2011, who will be aged between 65 and 74 on 5th April 2012, and who is not eligible to claim the married couples allowance. The effective tax rates applying to their employment, self-employment, pension or property income for 2011/12 are as follows:

First £9,940:	Nil
£9,940 to £24,000:	20%
£24,000 to: £28,930:	30%
£28,930 to £42,475:	20%
Over £42,475:	As above

In our third scenario, we will consider an individual aged 75 or over on 5th April 2012, who is eligible to claim married couples allowance. The effective tax rates applying to their employment, self-employment, pension or property income for 2011/12 are:

First £10,090:	Nil
£10,090 to £17,385:	10%
£17,385 to £24,000:	20%
£24,000 to £29,230:	30%
£29,230 to £38,220:	25%
£38,220 to £42,475:	20%
Over £42,475:	As above

(I know a lot of very sharp people over 75, but it does still seem pretty odd that the most complex set of tax rates that we have, with no less than ten different rate bands, is reserved for this age group!)

The total tax liability arising under each of these scenarios may be summarised as follows:

Income	Woman Aged 60-64 (Scenario 1)	Individual Aged 65-74 (Scenario 2)	Married Person Over 75 (Scenario 3)
£10,000	£505	£12	£0
£20,000	£2,505	£2,012	£1,253
£30,000	£4,505	£4,505	£3,814
£40,000	£6,505	£6,505	£6,225
£50,000	£10,010	£10,010	£9,730
£100,000	£30,010	£30,010	£29,730
£150,000	£53,000	£53,000	£52,720
£200,000	£78,000	£78,000	£77,720

Headings are for reference only. Please refer to the text above for a detailed description of each scenario.

Investment Income Received by Older Taxpayers

The tax rates applying to interest and other savings income not classed as dividends received by older taxpayers are generally the same as for other income, as set out above.

The only differences arise in the limited circumstances where the 10% starting rate band applies. Under these circumstances, the effective tax rates for our three scenarios set out above would differ only in the following respects:

Scenario 1:   £7,475 to £10,035:   10%

Scenario 2:   £9,940 to £12,500:   10%

Scenario 3:   £10,090 to £12,650:   Nil

The effective tax rates applying to dividends received by older taxpayers are generally the same as for other taxpayers except that the withdrawal of age-related allowances can create an effective tax charge on a small band of income over the 'income limit' where the individual is also in receipt of other types of income.

The position here is rather complex, as it depends on the exact mix of income received by the individual. Generally, however, for our scenarios above, the maximum extents of these bands are as follows:

Scenario 1:   Not Applicable

Scenario 2:   £24,000 to £28,437:   11.1%

Scenario 3:   £24,000 to £28,707:   11.1%
               £28,707 to £36,798:   5.56%

In some limited circumstances, an effective marginal rate of 16.7% can arise in place of the 11.1% rate on a band of dividend income up to £4,608 in total. However, this can only apply where the individual has employment, self-employment, pension and property income of less than £12,650 in total.

Female State Retirement Age

The state retirement age for women is now being increased and will reach 65 on 6th April 2020.

Women born between 6th April 1950 and 5th April 1955 will reach state retirement age approximately two months after 6th April 2010 for every month after 5th April 1950 that they were born.

This is done as follows:

   i)   Calculate the number of months, or part months, between 5th April 1950 and the woman's date of birth.
   ii) Add this number of months to the date of her 60th birthday.
   iii) Her retirement date is the last 6th of the month preceding the date derived under (ii).

For example, a woman born on 13th January 1951 was born between nine and ten months after 5th April 1950. We therefore add ten months to her 60th birthday. The result of this is 13th November 2011.

Her retirement date is the previous 6th of the month: 6th November 2011.

The following table summarises women's state retirement dates falling during 2011/12:

Date of Birth	State Retirement Date
6th October to 5th November 1950	6th May 2011
6th November to 5th December 1950	6th July 2011
6th December 1950 to 5th January 1951	6th September 2011
6th January to 5th February 1951	6th November 2011
6th February to 5th March 1951	6th January 2012
6th March to 5th April 1951	6th March 2012

Women born after 5th April 1950 will continue to be liable for National Insurance on employment or self-employment income until they reach their revised state retirement age under these rules (see above for further details of the exact point at which liability ceases).

The Government is proposing to increase the state retirement age for both genders to 66 in the near future. For men, the increase is likely to take place within the next few years; for women it will not take place until at least 2020.

Chapter 2

Future Tax Changes

Whilst this guide is primarily concerned with planning for the current tax year ending 5th April 2012, it is worth us giving some consideration to the changes which may lie ahead.

It is important to understand that any proposed future changes to the tax system are just that: proposals. Until a proposal is enacted by Parliament, there is always the possibility that it will be amended or even scrapped. This uncertainty is always with us, at any time, but is currently exacerbated by the fact that we have a Coalition Government.

In this chapter, we will look at the future tax changes currently proposed, up to and including the announcements in the Budget on 23rd March 2011.

Whilst the future is an uncertain place, current proposals are the best indication we have of what is likely to happen. We should therefore give them some consideration, albeit with the major proviso that further changes are highly likely.

The future tax changes currently proposed are as follows:

- The Income Tax personal allowance for individuals aged under 65 is to be increased to £8,105 for 2012/13
- The personal allowance is to be further increased to a target level of £10,000 by the end of the current Parliament (which the Government seems to be assuming will be in 2015/16)
- The higher rate Income Tax threshold for both 2012/13 and 2013/14 will be held at its 2011/12 level of £42,475
- As a result, the basic rate band for 2012/13 will be reduced to £34,370
- The National Insurance upper earnings limit is to continue to be aligned with the higher rate Income Tax threshold
- All other National Insurance thresholds and weekly contribution rates will be increased in line with the Consumer Prices Index (instead of the Retail Prices Index) from 2012/13 onwards; except for the employer's

secondary contribution threshold which will continue to increase in line with the Retail Prices Index for the life of this Parliament

- The main rate of Corporation Tax (currently 26%) is to be reduced by 1% on 1st April each year until 2014, thus reducing it to 23% by the end of this period
- The Inheritance Tax nil rate band is to remain at £325,000 until at least 5th April 2015
- All annual inflationary increases to direct tax thresholds, allowances and rate bands will be moved across to the Consumer Prices Index (instead of the Retail Prices Index) by 2016/17

A 'freeze' should be regarded as a change because it means that the effects of inflation are being ignored.

We will return to the proposals regarding Corporation Tax and Inheritance Tax later in the guide. For the time being, we will concentrate on the implications of the proposals for Income Tax and National Insurance.

The change to using the Consumer Prices Index as the inflation measure for direct tax thresholds, allowances and rate bands, is far more significant than it may at first appear.

This is because the Consumer Prices Index excludes housing costs (mortgage payments, rent, etc.) and therefore generally runs at a much lower level than the Retail Prices Index. The compound effect over many years of using the lower inflation measure will be quite considerable and, over time, will effectively result in much higher tax bills for all of us.

The Government's own estimates of the additional tax raised by moving primary National Insurance alone over to the Consumer Prices Index rise from a mere £105m in 2012/13 to over £1 billion by 2015/16!

Future Tax Forecasts

At this point, it is worth us examining what the current proposals will do for the various categories of taxpayer which we examined in Chapter 1. To do this, we must first make some forecasts of our own regarding the likely shape of the Income Tax and National

Insurance system over the next few years. For the purposes of our forecasts, I am going to assume as follows:

i) All of the proposed future changes detailed above will take place (remember this is only an assumption).

ii) The Income Tax personal allowance for individuals aged under 65 will be increased in approximately equal steps each year from 2013/14 to 2015/16 in order to reach £10,000 by the end of that period.

iii) The threshold at which the personal allowance begins to be withdrawn will remain at its current level of £100,000.

iv) The 'super tax' threshold will remain at its current level of £150,000.

v) Subject to the above points, all other Income Tax allowances, bands and thresholds will increase in line with Retail Prices Index inflation at an estimated rate of 5.6% for 2012/13 and 3.5% thereafter.

vi) National Insurance thresholds and weekly contribution rates will increase in line with Consumer Prices Index inflation at an estimated rate of 4.5% for 2012/13 and 2.5% thereafter, except where noted to the contrary above.

Whilst I have tried to make my assumptions as logical as possible based on the information currently available to us, they are still just assumptions. Any of the proposals announced to date could be changed and my other assumptions may be superseded by future announcements. In essence, therefore, the forecasts which follow are simply my 'best guess' based on the information available at the time of writing.

My forecasts are also based on the assumption that the 50% 'super tax' rate will remain in force for the foreseeable future. There are rumours, however, that the 'super tax' rate may be abolished as soon as 2013/14. Indeed, the Chancellor has made it clear that he regards the 50% rate as a temporary measure: just as Pitt the Younger regarded Income Tax itself as a 'temporary measure' when he introduced it in 1799!

Readers will therefore have to make up their own mind about the life expectancy of the 50% 'super tax'.

Future Tax Rates and Allowances

The forecast future Income Tax and National Insurance thresholds, allowances and rate bands for the tax years 2012/13 to 2015/16, based on the assumptions above, are set out in Appendices A and B. Let's now look at how these forecasts affect the tax paid by different classes of taxpayers.

Employment Income

The estimated total Income Tax and National Insurance paid by employed earners over the next three years is shown in the table below. The position for the current year is also included for the purposes of comparison.

Annual Earnings	Tax & NI 2011/12	Tax & NI 2012/13	Tax & NI 2013/14	Tax & NI 2014/15
£10,000	£838	£672	£524	£374
£20,000	£4,038	£3,872	£3,724	£3,574
£30,000	£7,238	£7,072	£6,924	£6,774
£40,000	£10,438	£10,272	£10,124	£9,974
£50,000	£14,391	£14,225	£14,076	£13,814
£75,000	£24,891	£24,725	£24,576	£24,314
£100,000	£35,391	£35,225	£35,076	£34,814
£150,000	£59,381	£59,467	£59,570	£59,560
£200,000	£85,381	£85,467	£85,570	£85,560

Employer's secondary National Insurance at 13.8% is not included in the above figures.

Self-Employment

The position for self-employment income is broadly similar, except that the primary rate of National Insurance will be 9% rather than the 12% applying to employment income and there is also a further small amount payable in Class 2 National Insurance whenever the earnings exceed the 'small earnings exception' limit.

Hence, the main differences in the combined Income Tax and National Insurance rates between self-employed and employed earners over the next three years will be the fact that the total rate applying to income falling into the basic rate band will be 29%, rather than 32%, and the additional payment of around £140 in Class 2 National Insurance each year.

Taking all of this into account, the forecast total Income Tax and National Insurance payable on self-employment income over the next three years is as shown in the table below. (The position for the current year is again included for comparison.)

Annual Earnings	Tax & NI 2011/12	Tax & NI 2012/13	Tax & NI 2013/14	Tax & NI 2014/15
£10,000	£885	£737	£599	£460
£20,000	£3,785	£3,637	£3,499	£3,360
£30,000	£6,685	£6,537	£6,399	£6,260
£40,000	£9,585	£9,437	£9,299	£9,160
£50,000	£13,463	£13,315	£13,177	£12,892
£75,000	£23,963	£23,815	£23,677	£23,392
£100,000	£34,463	£34,315	£34,177	£33,892
£150,000	£58,453	£58,557	£58,671	£58,638
£200,000	£84,453	£84,557	£84,671	£84,638

Landlords

Rental income continues to be exempt from all classes of National Insurance. The estimated Income Tax payable on rental income over the next three years is shown in the table below, together with the usual current year comparison.

Income	Tax 2011/12	Tax 2012/13	Tax 2013/14	Tax 2014/15
£10,000	£505	£379	£253	£127
£20,000	£2,505	£2,379	£2,253	£2,127
£30,000	£4,505	£4,379	£4,253	£4,127
£40,000	£6,505	£6,379	£6,253	£6,127
£50,000	£10,010	£9,884	£9,758	£9,407
£75,000	£20,010	£19,884	£19,758	£19,407
£100,000	£30,010	£29,884	£29,758	£29,407
£150,000	£53,000	£53,126	£53,252	£53,153
£200,000	£78,000	£78,126	£78,252	£78,153

Investment Income

As explained in Chapter 1, investment income is taxed in different ways according to its type. Currently, for Income Tax purposes, investment income may be broken down into three main types: interest, dividends and 'large' foreign dividends from shareholdings of 10% or more in a company located in a 'tax haven'.

All types of investment income are exempt from all classes of National Insurance.

In the tables which follow, we will make the assumption that the taxpayer receives only one type of income.

Forecast Income Tax on Interest Income

Income	Tax 2011/12	Tax 2012/13	Tax 2013/14	Tax 2014/15
£10,000	£253	£190	£127	£64
£20,000	£2,249	£2,108	£1,972	£1,836
£30,000	£4,249	£4,108	£3,972	£3,836
£40,000	£6,249	£6,108	£5,972	£5,836
£50,000	£9,754	£9,613	£9,477	£9,116
£75,000	£19,754	£19,613	£19,477	£19,116
£100,000	£29,754	£29,613	£29,477	£29,116
£150,000	£52,744	£52,855	£52,971	£52,862
£200,000	£77,744	£77,855	£77,971	£77,862

As explained in Chapter 1, the 10% starting rate continues to apply to interest income. In compiling the above table, it has been assumed that this will remain the case throughout the forecast period.

Forecast Income Tax on Dividend Income

Income	Tax 2011/12	Tax 2012/13	Tax 2013/14	Tax 2014/15
£30,000	£0	£0	£0	£0
£40,000	£443	£443	£443	£190
£50,000	£2,943	£2,943	£2,943	£2,690
£75,000	£9,193	£9,193	£9,193	£8,940
£100,000	£16,693	£16,693	£16,693	£16,440
£150,000	£31,292	£31,433	£31,575	£31,464
£200,000	£49,347	£49,489	£49,631	£49,519

The position for dividends is, as ever, complicated by the one ninth tax credit which we looked at in Chapter 1. The amounts shown in the 'Income' column above represent the actual dividends received and do not include the tax credit.

As explained in Chapter 1, the one ninth tax credit does not apply where the recipient owns 10% or more of the shares in the company and the company is located in a 'tax haven'. This will increase the Income Tax liability on any such dividends.

The Income Tax liability on any foreign dividends may be reduced by any available double tax relief.

Pensions

As before, the tax rates applying to pension income received by taxpayers aged under 65 will continue to be the same as for rental income (see above).

For those aged 65 and over, the additional age-related allowances will continue to apply to produce a slightly different situation.

Older Taxpayers

The following table shows the estimated Income Tax payable on employment, self-employment, pension or property income received by an individual aged between 65 and 74 at the end of the relevant tax year who is not eligible for the married couples allowance.

Income	Tax 2011/12	Tax 2012/13	Tax 2013/14	Tax 2014/15
£10,000	£12	£0	£0	£0
£20,000	£2,012	£1,900	£1,826	£1,748
£30,000	£4,505	£4,360	£4,196	£4,018
£40,000	£6,505	£6,379	£6,253	£6,127
£50,000	£10,010	£9,884	£9,758	£9,407
£75,000	£20,010	£19,884	£19,758	£19,407
£100,000	£30,010	£29,884	£29,758	£29,407
£150,000	£53,000	£53,126	£53,252	£53,153
£200,000	£78,000	£78,126	£78,252	£78,153

Women Over Retirement Age

The estimated Income Tax payable on employment, self-employment, pension or property income received by a woman over state retirement age but aged under 65 at the end of the relevant tax year and not eligible for the married couples allowance is as follows:

Income	Tax 2011/12	Tax 2012/13	Tax 2013/14	Tax 2014/15
£10,000	£505	£379	£253	£127
£20,000	£2,505	£2,379	£2,253	£2,127
£30,000	£4,505	£4,379	£4,253	£4,127
£40,000	£6,505	£6,379	£6,253	£6,127
£50,000	£10,010	£9,884	£9,758	£9,407
£75,000	£20,010	£19,884	£19,758	£19,407
£100,000	£30,010	£29,884	£29,758	£29,407
£150,000	£53,000	£53,126	£53,252	£53,153
£200,000	£78,000	£78,126	£78,252	£78,153

See Chapter 1 for details of female state retirement ages.

Planning for Tax Changes

Changes to the tax regime or changes in an individual's own personal circumstances frequently result in an anticipated change in the tax rate applying to that individual's income or capital gains.

Where the rate applying is set to decrease then this only adds more weight to the general philosophy that taxable income and gains should be deferred whenever legitimately possible.

Where, however, the rate applying is set to increase, there may be instances where it is actually beneficial to accelerate taxable income or capital gains in order to benefit from the lower rate currently applying. This is only worthwhile, however, where the current tax rate applying is lower than the future rate to such an extent that this will adequately compensate for the effective interest cost arising by accelerating the tax liability.

Furthermore, even in a situation which meets this criterion, it will usually only be worth accelerating taxable income or capital gains if it is reasonably certain that the income or gains are going to be taxable at a higher rate in the foreseeable future.

Nevertheless, opportunities frequently exist for those expecting income below the higher rate tax threshold (currently £42,475) this year, but over that threshold next year, to save tax by bringing income or capital gains forward.

Furthermore, the 'super tax' rate of 50% on income over £150,000 and withdrawal of personal allowances from those with income over £100,000 could mean that many other people may stand to make significant Income Tax savings by bringing income forward so that it falls into the current tax year.

For employment or self-employment income, we will also need to take National Insurance into account. This will reduce the savings for those making use of their basic rate tax band this year, but those savings will often still be worthwhile.

For example, a self-employed person expecting total income of around £30,000 this year, but around £50,000 next year, could save £130 for each £1,000 of income they are able to bring forward into this year (until they reduce next year's income down to the higher rate tax threshold). They would pay just £290 in Income Tax and National Insurance on each £1,000 of accelerated income this year instead of £420 next year, making it well worth suffering the earlier tax bill.

A person expecting total income between £114,950 and £140,000 this year, but over £150,000 next year, could possibly save £1,000 in Income Tax by bringing £10,000 of income forward into 2011/12. This would generally be enough to compensate for having to pay the £4,200 tax due on this income a year earlier.

Those anticipating income between £100,000 and £116,210 next year could save even more. If their expected income this year lies outside this bracket, they may save tax at an effective rate of up to 20% by bringing some of their income forward.

For example, let us suppose that an employee with a current salary of £90,000 (and no other income) is due both a payrise and a bonus in April 2012. The payrise will take their salary to £100,000 and the bonus of £10,000 can be taken on either 5th or 6th April.

By taking the bonus on the earlier date, the employee would save £2,000 in Income Tax.

What's more, since the bonus falls under the PAYE system, this would only accelerate the tax payment by a month. That's equivalent to a £2,000 return on £4,200 invested for one month!

Most of the cases where opportunities exist to legitimately accelerate or defer taxable income arise in the context of people in business and we will return to this subject in more detail in Chapter 7. Capital gains are covered in Chapter 12.

It nevertheless remains worthwhile for everyone to bear in mind the principles set out above, namely:

It is generally beneficial to defer taxable income or capital gains whenever legitimately possible but, in some instances, it may sometimes be better to accelerate taxable income or gains where a future increase in the applicable taxation rate is anticipated.

When to Accelerate Income

The tables below indicate the main situations where savings in Income Tax and National Insurance of 10% or more can be generated where it is possible to accelerate income so that it falls into 2011/12 instead of 2012/13.

The tax brackets used for 2012/13 are based on current Government proposals and the forecast assumptions set out earlier in this chapter. The projected tax savings are based on the assumptions that all current proposals do come into force and the individual concerned will be below state retirement age on 5th April 2013.

Wealth Warning

Increasing total income for 2011/12 may result in increased Capital Gains Tax liabilities where the individual has capital gains arising in the year and has not already fully utilised their basic rate Income Tax band. See Chapter 12 for further details.

Table 1: Savings for those paying Basic Rate Income Tax in 2011/12

Expected Total Income 2011/12	Expected Total Income 2012/13	Potential saving through acceleration of income
£7,475 to £42,475	£42,475 to £100,000 OR £116,210 to £150,000	10% on employment income 13% on self-employment income 20% on interest, pensions or rental income* 25% on dividends
£7,475 to £42,475	£100,000 to £116,210	30% on employment income 33% on self-employment income At least 37.5% on dividends 40% on interest, pensions or rental income*
£7,475 to £42,475	Over £150,000	20% on employment income 23% on self-employment income 30% on interest, pensions or rental income* 36.1% on dividends

* - Except for interest income in cases where existing income for 2011/12 is between £7,475 and £10,035. In these cases, the potential savings are increased by an additional 10% (e.g. 30% instead of 20%, etc).

Table 2: Savings for those paying Higher Rate Income Tax in 2011/12

Expected Total Income 2011/12	Expected Total Income 2012/13	Potential saving through acceleration of income
£42,475 to £100,000 OR £114,950 to £150,000	£100,000 to £116,210	At least 12.5% on dividends 20% on interest, pensions or rental income 20% on employment or self-employment income
£42,475 to £100,000 OR £114,950 to £150,000	Over £150,000	10% on interest, pensions or rental income 10% on employment or self-employment income 11.1% on dividends
Over £150,000	£100,000 to £116,210	10% on interest, pensions or rental income 10% on employment or self-employment income Up to 12.5% on dividends (depending on other income in 2012/13)

For dividend income, the 'expected total income' given in both of the above tables includes the one ninth tax credit.

Chapter 3

Investments That Will Save You Tax

Wealth Warning

In the next two chapters, we will consider the various forms of tax-advantaged investments currently available to help you reduce your current or future tax liabilities. The role of this guide is to make you aware of the types of investments available and their tax implications. All forms of investment carry an inherent degree of risk. We strongly recommend that you always consult a financial adviser before making any of the investments described here.

Individual Savings Accounts (ISAs)

The simplest piece of basic tax planning is to make full use of your annual ISA allowance. Investments in ISAs are completely tax free for your lifetime – that means that all interest, dividends and capital gains within the ISA are totally exempt from tax.

Whilst these exemptions are a valuable tax-saving tool, investors should beware of one thing: ISAs are only exempt from tax during your lifetime. ISAs are **NOT** exempt from Inheritance Tax!

The annual ISA investment limits for 2011/12 are £5,340 for cash and £10,680 overall.

Each individual's ISA investments for 2011/12 may be made through cash deposits totalling up to £5,340 in a 'Cash ISA', together with other investments in quoted shares and securities within a separate 'Stocks and Shares ISA' up to an overall total of £10,680 for both ISA investments for the year.

For example, an individual could invest £5,340 in a Cash ISA plus a further £5,340 in a Stocks and Shares ISA.

Alternatively, they could invest just £1,000 in a Cash ISA and a further £9,680 in a Stocks and Shares ISA, or even just invest the whole £10,680 in a Stocks and Shares ISA.

An individual may open one new Cash ISA and one new Stocks and Shares ISA each tax year. Alternatively, they may continue to invest in a previous ISA but, once they have done so, they will be unable to open a new ISA of that type this year.

ISAs are available to all UK resident individuals aged 18 or over. Cash ISAs are also available to 16 and 17-year-old UK resident individuals, with the usual £5,340 investment limit.

Junior ISAs, for UK resident minors without a Child Trust Fund, are to be made available from Autumn 2011, but may be subject to a lower investment limit.

Interest, dividends and capital gains arising within an ISA may be re-invested and this does not count towards the annual investment limits. Funds may also be transferred between Cash ISAs or from existing Cash ISAs into shares and securities still held within the ISA regime.

Funds held in the form of shares and securities within the ISA regime may not be transferred into cash within the regime, however, so this is very much a 'one way street'.

If intending to transfer funds to a different ISA, it is important to ensure that this is treated as a transfer and not as a closure or withdrawal. Funds withdrawn from the ISA regime lose their tax-favoured status.

Note that some ISAs do not accept transfers and some may charge a penalty for early withdrawals.

Whilst the bank may sometimes make a commercial charge for early withdrawals, there is no 'exit charge' under the ISA regime itself. However, it is important to remember that funds withdrawn may not be reinvested once the annual investment limit has been reached.

Example

George pays £445 each month into his Cash ISA. In March 2012, he withdraws £2,000 to use as spending money on a skiing holiday.

On George's return from holiday on 3rd April 2012, he finds that he has £800 left over from his spending money and he decides to put this back into his ISA. Unfortunately, however, he is unable to do so, as he has already used up his £5,340 investment limit through his regular monthly investments. The fact that the cash was withdrawn from the ISA in the first place makes no difference!

(George could put the extra money into his ISA on 6th April but, again, that would use up part of his 2012/13 investment limit.)

Child Trust Funds

Every child born in the UK between 1st September 2002 and 31st December 2010 should have a Child Trust Fund.

Parents, family and friends of any child eligible for a Child Trust Fund may put up to an additional £1,200 in total per tax year into the child's Child Trust Fund account. Monies within the Fund will be invested in a long-term investment account to grow free from Income Tax or Capital Gains Tax, rather like an ISA.

On maturity, the funds within the Child Trust Fund may be transferred to an ISA in the child's name. However, the first such funds will not mature for almost a decade!

Venture Capital Trusts (VCTs)

Venture Capital Trusts are a specialised type of tax-advantaged investment vehicle, allowing a broad range of investors to pool their resources and invest in new or developing business ventures.

For the tax year 2011/12, up to £200,000 may be invested in Venture Capital Trusts, generally providing Income Tax relief at the rate of 30% of the amount invested.

To be precise, the relief given is equal to the lower of:

i)   30% of the amount invested (up to a maximum investment of £200,000), and
ii)   The amount which reduces the individual's total Income Tax liability to nil.

Example

During the year ending 5ᵗʰ April 2012, Cedric will receive a salary of £120,000. This will give him a total Income Tax liability for 2011/12 of £41,000.

Cedric wishes to invest £200,000 in a Venture Capital Trust. The maximum relief available for such an investment, at 30%, would be £60,000. However, this exceeds Cedric's 2011/12 Income Tax liability and if he was to make the whole of this investment before 6ᵗʰ April 2012, he would be wasting almost £20,000 of potential relief.

What Cedric should do, therefore, is invest no more than £136,666 in the Venture Capital Trust before the end of the 2011/12 tax year on 5ᵗʰ April 2012 and, if he so wishes, invest the balance after that date, so that it falls into 2012/13.

This way, Cedric will be able to get the full £60,000 worth of relief on his investment.

Note that the relief for Venture Capital Trust investments is given only against Income Tax. No relief is available against Capital Gains Tax or against National Insurance of any class.

Had Cedric been a self-employed taxpayer on the same level of income, his maximum Venture Capital Trust relief for 2011/12 would have remained unaltered, even though he would have been paying £4,723 in Class 4 National Insurance.

Venture Capital Trusts may currently only invest in qualifying trading companies with gross assets not exceeding £7m prior to the investment being made (and not exceeding £8m immediately after that investment). The Government is proposing to increase the £7m investment limit to £15m from 6ᵗʰ April 2012, subject to state aid approval from the European Commission.

Investee companies must also have fewer than 50 employees. The Government is also proposing to increase this limit, to fewer than 250 employees, from 6th April 2012 (again, subject to state aid approval from the European Commission).

Venture Capital Trusts can no longer be used to provide Capital Gains Tax reinvestment relief, which was abolished in 2004.

Venture Capital Trust shares issued after 5th April 2006 must be held for at least five years or the initial tax relief will be withdrawn. (A minimum holding period of three years applied to Venture Capital Trust shares issued between 6th April 2000 and 5th April 2006.)

Dividends on qualifying ordinary shares in a Venture Capital Trust are tax free.

Capital gains arising on the sale of such shares after the expiry of the minimum holding period referred to above are also tax free.

'Qualifying' in this context means that the original investment qualified for Income Tax relief, as explained above. (Had Cedric invested the whole £200,000 in 2011/12, all of his shares would have **qualified** for relief, notwithstanding the fact that the amount of relief given would have been restricted.)

Enterprise Investment Scheme (EIS) Shares

Investments in Enterprise Investment Scheme shares up to a specified annual limit each tax year are eligible for Income Tax relief. For 2011/12, relief is given at the lower of 30% or the individual's own total Income Tax liability. For earlier years, the maximum rate of relief was 20%.

The current annual investment limit is £500,000. The Government proposes to increase this to £1m from 2012/13 onwards.

Enterprise Investment Scheme investments may also be carried back for Income Tax relief in the previous tax year. The amount eligible for relief in each year will be restricted to the annual investment limit for that year and the rate of relief given will be the applicable rate for that year.

In effect, this means that a person who did not make any Enterprise Investment Scheme investments in 2010/11 can get tax relief on an investment of up to £1m made in 2011/12. Full relief would be obtained by carrying £500,000 back for relief in 2010/11, leaving the remaining £500,000 to be relieved in the current year.

It is important to note, however, that only the £500,000 relieved in 2011/12 would attract relief at a maximum of 30%, with the relief on the £500,000 carried back to 2010/11 restricted to a maximum of 20%. The total relief produced by this investment would thus amount to a maximum of £250,000.

The carry back facility can also be used to maximise the Income Tax relief obtained on smaller investments.

Example

Margaret has total income of £90,000 in both 2010/11 and 2011/12, giving her Income Tax liabilities of £25,930 and £26,010 respectively. In November 2011, she invests £200,000 in Enterprise Investment Scheme shares.

The most tax relief that Margaret can obtain in 2011/12 alone is £26,010: equivalent to relief at 30% on an investment of £86,700. However, by carrying back £113,300 (£200,000 - £86,700) of her investment for relief in 2010/11, she can also obtain a further £22,660 of relief (£113,300 x 20%), giving her total relief of £48,670.

Furthermore, as £22,660 of Margaret's tax relief is obtained a year earlier, this will give her either a reduction in tax due, or a tax repayment, on 31st January 2012.

As we can see from the example, the carry back facility has two major benefits: it can be used to increase the overall amount of tax relief due and can also be used to accelerate relief by a year. The second benefit alone is often reason enough to carry back, although this is not the case this year, as the amount carried back only obtains relief at 20% instead of 30%.

There is a minimum investment limit of £500 per tax year and this applies to each Enterprise Investment Scheme company in which a taxpayer invests. However, where the taxpayer invests through an approved investment fund, the minimum investment limit does not apply.

Enterprise Investment Scheme shares are issued by a single, qualifying, unquoted, trading company. As with Venture Capital Trust investments, the company issuing the Enterprise Investment Scheme shares must have gross assets not exceeding £7m prior to the share issue (and not exceeding £8m immediately after the issue) and must have fewer than 50 employees. The proposed increases to these limits from 6th April 2012 for Venture Capital Trust investments, as discussed above, will also apply to the Enterprise Investment Scheme.

To obtain Income Tax relief, the investor must not be connected with the company issuing the shares. An investor is generally deemed to be connected with the company for this purpose when they own 30% or more of the share capital in the company **after** the Enterprise Investment Scheme shares are issued.

Capital Gains Tax reinvestment relief may still be obtained where appropriate, however; even when the investor is connected with the company (see Chapter 12 for further details).

Where the investor is not connected with the company issuing the Enterprise Investment Scheme shares, the total combined Income Tax and Capital Gains Tax savings could now total up to 58% of the amount invested (48% where the gain to be deferred arose before 23rd June 2010).

Readers must bear in mind, however, that investment in an unconnected Enterprise Investment Scheme company is inherently risky and professional advice from a financial adviser is essential when choosing such investments.

Products are available which reduce the overall level of risk by pooling several investors' funds and investing them in a portfolio of Enterprise Investment Scheme shares issued by a range of companies.

Enterprise Investment Scheme shares must be issued wholly for cash and must be held for at least three years (sometimes longer). The issuing company must also carry on a 'qualifying trade' (broadly one which is not property-based) throughout this period.

The Income Tax relief on the initial investment will be withdrawn if any of these conditions are breached.

Any capital gain arising on the sale of Enterprise Investment Scheme shares which initially qualified for Income Tax relief, as described above, is exempt from Capital Gains Tax. This exemption is also lost if the Income Tax relief is withdrawn.

Conversely, a capital loss on sale of Enterprise Investment Scheme shares remains allowable, although it must be reduced by the amount of Income Tax relief given on the initial investment.

Note that it is only the capital gain on the Enterprise Investment Scheme shares themselves which may be exempt. Gains held over on reinvestment into Enterprise Investment Scheme shares will become chargeable to Capital Gains Tax on a sale of those shares at any time.

Further Investment Limits

Under a similar scheme to the Enterprise Investment Scheme, companies may make tax-advantaged investments in other qualifying trading companies. This other scheme is known as the Corporate Venturing Scheme.

Companies issuing shares under the Enterprise Investment Scheme or the Corporate Venturing Scheme, or in which investments are made by a Venture Capital Trust, may not raise total new capital of more than £2m in any twelve month period under the three schemes taken together. The Government proposes to increase this limit to £10m from 6th April 2012, subject to state aid approval from the European Commission.

There are further additional detailed rules regarding investments under these schemes, some of which were recently amended.

Friendly Societies

Due to a little known quirk in the tax system, individuals aged between 16 and 74 may invest up to £25 per month in tax-exempt savings policies issued by friendly societies. Not only do these policies provide life cover but they also provide an additional opportunity to make tax-free investments. Typically the funds are invested in quoted shares and securities.

Investments in friendly societies do not need to be taken into account when considering whether the taxpayer has utilised their annual ISA investment limits.

The tax-exempt savings policies run for a period of ten years and may then be 'cashed in' free from Income Tax or Capital Gains Tax.

Receiving Interest Gross

A number of accounts are now available which will pay interest gross without deduction of basic rate Income Tax. Typically, these accounts are accessed through an intermediary, such as a stockbroker. It is important to remember that the interest received on such accounts remains taxable. The full amount of tax due on the interest must ultimately be paid through the self-assessment system.

The receipt of gross interest does, however, represent a considerable cashflow advantage. Instead of suffering basic rate Income Tax at source, the taxpayer will retain the full amount of interest received and should not have to pay the tax arising on this income for at least another ten months, possibly up to 22 months (subject to the comments regarding collection of tax through PAYE in Chapter 5 below).

Investment Bonds

Investment bonds provide the opportunity to accumulate income in a form which is treated as capital growth and not taxed until the funds are realised. This is achieved by structuring the bonds as a type of life insurance policy, although the insurance cover is often quite a small element of the investment.

Furthermore, for suitable qualifying investments, up to 5% of the initial capital invested may be withdrawn each year free from tax. This enables the investor to receive what is, in effect, a tax free income stream whilst at the same time the balance of their fund continues to appreciate in value within a tax-free environment.

Partnership and Other Trading Losses

A number of structures have been developed over the last few years to give investors 'sideways loss relief' for investments in partnerships and other trading entities. The most successful of these schemes have undoubtedly been film partnership investments and we will return to these shortly.

In principle, these schemes work by enabling the investor to claim partnership or other trading losses and to set these off against their other income in the same tax year. This provides effective tax relief at the investor's highest marginal rate of tax.

The beauty of these schemes lies in the fact that the loss claimed is usually only (or mostly) a technical loss for tax purposes, generally due to the availability of special allowances in the underlying trade, and not a true economic loss. Hence the investor will generally get their money back in the end!

Unfortunately, recent anti-avoidance legislation has somewhat curtailed the tax benefits of these investments.

The first attack came with legislation specifically targeted at 'non-active' partners, i.e. investors who are not actively involved in the partnership trade. For this purpose, a partner is generally classed as 'non-active' if they spend an average of less than ten hours per week engaged in the partnership's trading activities.

Firstly, the total cumulative amount of loss which a non-active partner may claim is restricted to the amount of capital which they have invested in the partnership.

Secondly, an annual limit of £25,000 has been placed on claims for partnership loss relief by non-active partners. This limit applies to the total claims made by a taxpayer in any tax year in respect of all partnerships in which they are a non-active partner.

Furthermore, for most investments made by non-active partners after 1st March 2007, a further rule excludes any capital contributed to the partnership where the main purpose, or one of the main purposes, behind the contribution is to enable the partner to claim sideways loss relief.

Where this rule applies to capital invested after 1st March 2007, the investment cannot be counted towards the amount of capital invested by the non-active partner for the purposes of calculating their maximum cumulative claim for partnership loss relief under the first rule above.

Any trading losses made by a 'non-active sole trader' must also be included within the amounts covered by the £25,000 limit. Personally, I find the term 'non-active sole trader' to be as much of a contradiction in terms as an 'honest politician', but it is again to be taken to mean someone who spends less than ten hours per week engaged in trading activities.

Relief is barred altogether for trading losses made by a 'non-active sole trader' as a result of arrangements made on or after 12th March 2008 for tax avoidance purposes.

Clearly, the various restrictions introduced in the last few years are aimed at preventing investors from gaining any tax advantage through investments structured as trading partnerships or sole trades. It is therefore essential to get professional advice on the tax position when considering any such investments.

It is to be hoped that these loss relief restrictions will not affect any genuine trading situations, although the rules are drawn very widely and I do fear that some 'innocents' will indeed be caught.

Film Relief

Film partnerships and other investments qualifying for film relief continue to enjoy significant tax advantages, as none of the restrictions on 'sideways loss relief' described above apply where a partnership or other trading loss is derived from 'relevant film-related expenditure'.

Lloyds Underwriters

Lloyds underwriters are also exempt from the restrictions on 'sideways loss relief' referred to above.

Business Premises Renovation Allowances

The Business Premises Renovation Allowance provides immediate 100% relief, at the investor's highest marginal rate of tax, for qualifying expenditure on the renovation or conversion of vacant commercial property in designated 'assisted areas' which is then brought back into business use.

The property must have been vacant for at least a year and certain types of business use are excluded from the relief. The new business use does not need to be the same as the property's previous use, however, and could include offices or shops.

The relief was originally scheduled to cease to apply after April 2012 but has now been extended for a further five years, meaning that expenditure incurred up until 11th April 2017 may now qualify.

Details of designated 'assisted areas' can be found in the Assisted Areas Order SI 2007/107.

Chapter 4

Pension Saving: How to Get a Much Bigger Tax Deduction

Introduction and Warning

Before we dive into the tax regime for pension contributions, it is important to remember that pension schemes are a form of investment and, as such, carry a degree of risk. The warning given at the beginning of Chapter 3 therefore applies equally here and I would recommend that anyone seeking to undertake pension planning, or tax planning involving pensions, should take independent professional advice.

Throughout 2009/10 and 2010/11, pension planning was hampered by some rather draconian 'anti-forestalling rules' introduced by the previous Government. Thankfully, the measures which these rules were designed to stop us forestalling never saw the light of day, as they were cancelled by the new Coalition Government before they were even implemented!

Instead, however, we do now have some much tighter restrictions on the total permitted level of qualifying, tax-advantaged, pension investments for each individual.

The new restrictions generally apply from 6th April 2011 although, in certain circumstances, pension contributions made from 14th October 2010 onwards may be affected. Furthermore, an individual's pension saving history going back as far as 6th April 2007 could potentially impact on the level of contributions which they are able to make in 2011/12.

Having said all that, the new restrictions will not affect the majority of pension investors and, furthermore, a detailed understanding of the new rules will also enable many others to achieve the desired result with a little careful planning.

The last few years have also witnessed a great deal of rumour concerning the abolition of higher-rate tax relief on pension contributions. Thankfully, these rumours have proven unfounded (so far, at least) and the likelihood of higher-rate tax relief being abolished appears to be much diminished under the new Coalition Government: especially since they have now put alternative restrictions in place.

Nevertheless, an abolition of higher-rate tax relief at some point in the future cannot be completely ruled out so, for those with plenty of surplus cash (a rare breed, I appreciate), it could be a case of 'making hay while the sun shines' and maximising the value of their pension contributions this year.

On the other hand, the current economic climate means that there will be many individuals for whom any pension contributions made this year are of far less value than in the past.

The situation we face today is therefore a maze of conflicting considerations where some people face restrictions on the amount of pension contributions that they are able to make, others might be well advised to defer any pension contributions, and we all live under the (admittedly somewhat diminished) shadow of a potential future ban on higher rate tax relief.

We will take a detailed look at all the tax planning pitfalls and opportunities created by this 'maze' later in this chapter. Before then, however, let's look at the current pension regime and its tax implications for the majority of investors today.

Pension Contributions

Subject to the restrictions discussed later in this chapter, personal pension contributions generally attract tax relief at the investor's highest marginal rate of Income Tax or, as we shall see in Chapter 9, possibly even more.

Basic rate tax relief at 20% is given at source. Hence, a contribution of £80 is actually worth £100, as HM Revenue and Customs will add the additional £20 directly into the investor's scheme (provided that the conditions for relief, as set out below, are met). It is important to note that it is the 'gross' contribution of £100 which is taken into account for all tax purposes, including the allowances described below.

Any further relief due is given through the Income Tax self-assessment system, or through the investor's PAYE code. If claiming relief via the PAYE system, it is vital to check that the correct amount of relief is being given, as mistakes are, to say the least, common!

Some old-style retirement annuity premiums are still paid gross (with no tax relief at source) and all tax relief must be claimed through the self-assessment system or via PAYE codes.

The two main tenets of the current system for pension contributions are the annual allowance and the lifetime allowance.

The Annual Allowance

The annual allowance represents the maximum amount qualifying for tax relief which may be added to an individual's total pension funds during the year. This includes contributions made by the individual themselves, contributions made on their behalf, and any increases in the individual's entitlement under 'defined benefit' or 'final salary' schemes (we will look at how such increases are measured later in this chapter).

It is important to note, however, that, for the purposes of the annual allowance, we do not count the pension contributions made during the tax year: the annual allowance actually applies to pension scheme years (or 'pension input periods') ending during the tax year.

We will look at the implications of this in more detail a little later. For the time being, I will just refer to contributions made during the tax year for the sake of simplicity.

For 2011/12 onwards, the annual allowance has been drastically reduced to just £50,000. (The allowance for 2010/11 was £255,000.)

However, this reduction is not as drastic as it may, at first, appear. This is because, from 2011/12 onwards, any unused annual allowance for each of the three previous tax years may be added to the current year's annual allowance to produce a total 'available annual allowance' of up to £200,000.

There are two important restrictions to bear in mind when calculating the unused annual allowance for previous tax years:

- For this purpose, the annual allowance is deemed to have been £50,000 for each of the tax years 2008/9, 2009/10 and 2010/11.
- You can only count an unused annual allowance for a previous tax year *if* you were a member of a registered pension scheme during that year.

Contrary to previous advice from HM Revenue and Customs, the draft legislation introducing these rules now specifically states that you will have an unused annual allowance of £50,000 for any tax year in which you were a member of a registered pension scheme but did not make any pension contributions.

Tax Tip

Anyone who is not currently a member of a registered pension scheme should consider opening a scheme during the current tax year, even if they would not otherwise wish to make any pension contributions this year.

By opening a scheme with a small contribution by 5th April 2012, an unused annual allowance of almost £50,000 (i.e. £50,000 less the small contribution) will be available for use in any of the next three tax years.

If gross contributions of £50,000 or more have been made in any of the three previous tax years, there will be no unused annual allowance for that year.

From 2011/12 onwards, any contributions in excess of the annual allowance will use up part of the unused allowance in the previous three years, taking the earliest year first. Provided that the excess is covered by those unused annual allowances, however, there will be no restriction in the tax relief for the contributions made in the current year.

In other words, contributions made in the current tax year will attract full tax relief at the investor's highest marginal rate of tax provided that the total gross contributions in the year do not exceed the 'available annual allowance'.

Example

Kate has made gross pension contributions (including the 20% tax relief given at source) of £30,000 in each of the previous three tax years. This means that she has unused annual allowances of £20,000 for each year, or £60,000 in total. Adding this to her annual allowance of £50,000 for 2011/12, gives her an available annual allowance this year of £110,000.

Kate can therefore make net pension contributions of up to £88,000 in 2011/12, giving her up to £22,000 of basic rate tax relief at source and higher-rate tax relief through self-assessment or her PAYE code.

Let's say she actually makes total gross contributions in 2011/12 of £60,000 (or £48,000 net). This means that she uses up £10,000 of her unused annual allowance for the earliest year available: 2008/9.

She still has £10,000 of unused annual allowance for 2008/9 but, as it can only be carried forward three years, this is now effectively lost.

In 2012/13, Kate has unused annual allowances of £20,000 for 2009/10 and £20,000 for £2010/11, giving her a total available annual allowance of £90,000. This time, she makes total gross contributions of £85,000. This uses up all of her unused allowance for 2009/10 and £15,000 of her unused allowance for 2010/11.

In 2013/14, Kate has an unused annual allowance of just £5,000 for 2010/11 (remember she made full use of her annual allowances in 2011/12 and 2012/13). Adding this to her annual allowance of £50,000, gives her an available annual allowance of £55,000 for 2013/14.

Where gross contributions have not exceeded £50,000 in any of the previous three tax years, the 'available annual allowance' will be £200,000 less the total gross contributions made in those previous three years. In other cases, the position will differ, as we saw for Kate in both 2012/13 and 2013/14 in the example above.

The current guidance available is not clear when it comes to the issue of how to treat anyone who made total gross contributions in excess of £50,000 in 2009/10 or 2010/11, but less than £50,000 in 2008/9 or 2009/10. The question is whether the excess contributions in the later year are treated as having used up some of the unused allowance for the earlier year, thus leaving less unused allowances available in 2011/12. Anyone potentially affected by this uncertainty should seek professional advice.

Pension Input Periods

As explained above, the annual allowance applies to contributions made to pension schemes during scheme years, or 'pension input periods', ending during the tax year.

Furthermore, an investor paying contributions into a personal pension scheme may choose to end their scheme year early – i.e. at any time up to the anniversary of the date on which the scheme year began.

This provides an opportunity for some additional planning, as it effectively allows up to *six* annual allowances to be used almost immediately in some cases!

Example

David has been a member of a registered pension scheme for many years, although he has not made any contributions during scheme years ending after 5th April 2008.

David is employed as a trouble-shooter to help out the ailing Big Bank plc after it was almost ruined by Sir Greedy Badloss. As part of his contract, David is due a bonus of £500,000 if he is able to return the bank to profit for the year ending 31st December 2011. David succeeds in his task and is therefore paid his bonus on 22nd March 2012.

After Income Tax and National Insurance totalling 52%, David will receive a net bonus of £240,000. He immediately makes a net pension contribution of £160,000, which is equivalent to £200,000 after being grossed-up for basic rate tax relief.

As things stand, assuming that David has opened up a new pension scheme with this contribution, the scheme year will run until 22nd March 2013. However, David can elect to end the scheme year early, on 23rd March 2012. The scheme year now ends during 2011/12 and David's contribution uses up his available annual allowance of £200,000 for the year (see above).

On 24th March 2012, David makes another pension contribution of £40,000, equivalent to £50,000 after being grossed-up for basic rate tax relief. This falls into a new scheme year and is therefore permitted, as long as the new scheme year ends in 2012/13.

David ends the second scheme year on 6th April 2012 and then makes a third pension contribution of £40,000 on 7th April 2012. Once again, the contribution is permitted, as it falls into a new scheme year. This time, David allows the scheme year to run its course, so that it ends on 6th April 2013, falls into the 2013/14 tax year and he can use his 2013/14 annual allowance.

As we can see, with careful timing, an individual who has not made any pension savings since 2007/8, could potentially make gross contributions of up to £300,000 (or £240,000 net) within a few days and still obtain full tax relief.

Note, however, that anyone making such large contributions (or indeed any contributions) also needs to take care not to breach the lifetime allowance (see below).

Is It Worth It?

In our example above, David was able to plan his pension contributions in such a way that he did not breach the annual allowance. Subject to the lifetime allowance (see below), this means that he continued to enjoy full tax relief on all of his contributions.

In David's case, this was worth additional contributions totalling £60,000 which were paid into the tax-free environment of his pension scheme by the Government, plus a further £90,000 worth of tax relief (£300,000 at 30%: David is a 50% 'super tax' payer, but has already had 20% relief at source).

These are quite considerable benefits, but whether they are enough to warrant such large investments in a pension scheme is a matter of debate. Some people think that pensions are the 'best thing since sliced bread', others are put off by the numerous restrictions on withdrawals (these are being eased somewhat under current Government proposals, but pensions are still a lot more restricted than other forms of saving).

It must also be borne in mind that, after a maximum tax-free lump sum equal to 25% of the scheme value, the remainder of all future payments received from the scheme will be subject to Income Tax, as detailed in Chapters 1 and 2.

In the end, pension investments are a matter of personal choice and making any contributions, large or small, clearly demands detailed professional advice!

Annual Allowance Charges

Breaching the annual allowance leads to a complete loss of tax relief on the excess contributions. This is done by levying an 'annual allowance charge' which is equivalent to the amount of tax relief given, including the basic rate tax relief given at source.

Prior to 2011/12, the annual allowance charge was levied on the individual making the excess contributions (or on whose behalf the contributions were made) and was payable by 31st January following the tax year which those excess contributions related to.

Under current Government proposals, however, the charge will now generally be payable when the individual draws their pension benefits. Furthermore, individuals will sometimes be able to elect for the charge to be paid out of the pension fund itself.

Whilst these changes are welcome, annual allowance charges are still best avoided whenever possible!

Transitional Relief

There are transitional rules in place to prevent annual allowance charges from arising on gross contributions in excess of £50,000 (but not more than £255,000) made before 14th October 2010 but falling into scheme years ending during 2011/12.

Broadly speaking, the previous annual allowance of £255,000 will continue to apply to contributions made before 14th October 2010.

Those contributions will, however, count towards the available annual allowance in respect of further contributions made on or after 14th October 2010 and falling into scheme years ending during 2011/12.

We suggest that you seek professional advice if you think you may be affected.

The Lifetime Allowance

The lifetime allowance represents the maximum permitted value for all of an individual's qualifying pension savings. The standard lifetime allowance is currently £1.8m, but the Government proposes to reduce it to £1.5m from 6th April 2012.

A 25% tax charge is levied on any funds in excess of the lifetime allowance on the occasion of a 'benefit crystallisation event': generally when the individual is first paid a pension, buys an annuity, or makes an income drawdown.

Alternatively, the individual can withdraw some or all of the excess funds as a lump sum, although this is subject to an increased charge of 55%.

Either way, the scheme administrator is required to deduct the charge from the fund and pay it over to HM Revenue and Customs.

Those anticipating having pension funds in excess of the new reduced standard lifetime allowance of £1.5m may apply for a form of transitional protection, known as 'fixed protection'.

Anyone whose pension funds might have a total value in excess of the new reduced lifetime allowance at any time should therefore take specialist professional advice as soon as possible.

Valuing Your Pension Pot

It is important to remember that both the annual allowance and the lifetime allowance must be applied to each individual's *total* qualifying pension funds. This will include any element of foreign pension funds derived from contributions for which UK tax relief has been obtained.

An individual's total qualifying pension funds will also include any defined benefit or 'final salary' schemes.

Defined Benefit Schemes

For defined benefit, or 'final salary', schemes, a valuation factor of 16 is now used to measure the increase in the value of an individual's benefits under the scheme for the purposes of the annual allowance.

That increase is, however, adjusted for inflation, using the increase in the Consumer Prices Index for the relevant period (see below).

Any increase in additional lump sum benefits due under the scheme must also be taken into account, except where the lump sum is only available by commuting part of the pension.

If the increase in the value of the individual's benefits (together with any other pension contributions made in pension input periods ending in the same tax year) exceeds their available annual allowance, they will be subject to an annual allowance charge on the excess. In this case, the charge is equivalent to the Income Tax which would have been paid on an additional amount of income equal to the excess – hence it will generally be at 40% or 50%.

Example

In April 2011, Sandra is a senior manager with a salary of £70,000. She is also a member of a 'final salary' occupational pension scheme, providing her with a pension equal to 50% of her salary.

At the beginning of the scheme year ending on 31ˢᵗ March 2012, the value of Sandra's pension fund is calculated as £560,000, 16 times her anticipated pension.

Previous increases in her accrued benefits mean that Sandra has an available annual allowance for 2011/12 of £170,000.

In June 2011, Sandra is promoted to the Board of Directors and her salary is increased to £84,000. She also becomes eligible for the executive pension scheme, which provides a pension equal to two thirds of her salary.

The value of Sandra's pension fund has now leapt up to £896,000 (£84,000 x 2/3rds x 16).

To calculate the increase for the purposes of the annual allowance, however, we must index the value of Sandra's benefits at the beginning of the scheme year by a factor of 3.1% (see below).

The relevant increase in the value of Sandra's pension fund is therefore as follows:

Original opening value	*£560,000*
Indexed for inflation (at 3.1%)	*£577,360*
Closing value	*£896,000*
Relevant increase (£896,000 - £577,360)	*£318,640*

Unfortunately, this increase in the value of Sandra's pension fund still exceeds her available annual allowance by £148,640. This will give rise to an annual allowance charge of around £67,500.

Furthermore, if Sandra makes any contributions to another pension fund in a scheme year ending during 2011/12, she will face a further 50% tax charge on those contributions too.

There may be a simple way to reduce the excessive charges which Sandra faces.

If she and her employers agree to defer her entry into the executive pension scheme until 1st April 2012 (i.e. the beginning of the next scheme year), the deemed value of Sandra's pension fund at 31st March 2012 would only be £672,000 (£84,000 x ½ x 16).

The relevant increase for annual allowance purposes would thus be £94,640 (£672,000 - £577,360) which would easily be covered by Sandra's available annual allowance for 2011/12.

Assuming that Sandra had originally used £10,000 of her annual allowance in each of 2008/9, 2009/10 and 2010/11, she would have used up all her remaining annual allowance for 2008/9 and a further £4,640 of her annual allowance for 2009/10.

This would leave her with an available annual allowance for 2012/13 of £125,360 (£50,000 for 2012/13 + £40,000 for 2010/11 + £40,000 - £4,640 for 2009/10).

As we know, at the end of the next scheme year on 31st March 2013, the value of Sandra's pension fund under the executive pension scheme would be £896,000 (assuming that any further pay increase which she might be due is deferred until 1st April 2013).

Once again, we must index the opening value of her fund to reflect inflation measured by the Consumer Prices Index. This time, this is likely to be around 4.5%.

The relevant increase in the value of Sandra's fund for annual allowance purposes is therefore calculated as follows:

Original opening value	£672,000
Indexed for inflation (at 4.5%)	£702,240
Closing value	£896,000
Relevant increase (£896,000 - £702,240)	£193,760

This time, the increase only exceeds Sandra's available annual allowance by £68,400 (£193,760 - £125,360), leading to an annual allowance charge of around £27,500: about £40,000 less than previously.

Hence, as we can see, managing the increase in the value of a defined benefit scheme, so that it is spread over two (or more) scheme years, could lead to considerable savings in some cases.

Indexing Scheme Values

As explained above, the opening value of a defined benefit scheme is indexed by reference to the increase in the Consumer Prices Index in order to determine the relevant increase in the scheme's deemed value for annual allowance purposes.

The increase in the Consumer Prices Index which is used for this purpose is the increase for the twelve months up to the September preceding the relevant tax year.

The same indexing method (and valuation factor of 16) must also be used when calculating how much of the individual's annual allowance was used in the previous three tax years.

The increases in the Consumer Prices Index which are relevant to the annual allowance calculations required for 2011/12 are as follows:

2008/9	1.8%
2009/10	5.2%
2010/11	1.1%
2011/12	3.1%

Inflation is now running a little higher than in the period to September 2010, so the factor to be used for 2012/13 can reasonably be estimated at around 4.5%.

Valuing Defined Benefit Schemes for the Lifetime Allowance

For the purposes of the lifetime allowance, a defined benefit scheme is generally valued at 20 times the amount of annual pension initially payable under the scheme.

Any lump sum due under the scheme must be added to this value, except where the lump sum is only available by commuting part of the pension.

In Sandra's case above, she is currently due a pension of £56,000 (£84,000 x 2/3rds), so her pension fund is valued at £1,120,000 for the purposes of the lifetime allowance.

Like most other members of occupational pension schemes, Sandra would probably only need to be concerned about the lifetime allowance if her anticipated annual pension increased above £75,000.

The point at which the lifetime allowance becomes an issue will be lower, however, where the individual has an automatic right to an additional lump sum (i.e. without commuting part of their pension), or has other pension savings.

For example, someone who also has £300,000 invested in a personal pension would be exposed to the lifetime allowance charge if they were entitled to an occupational pension of more than £60,000.

Tax Relief for Pension Contributions

It is important to understand that there is no longer a direct link between the maximum amount of contributions which may actually be made and the maximum which will attract tax relief.

Individuals may, in fact, make unlimited contributions if they so desire, but, as explained above, they will incur penalty charges if they breach either the lifetime allowance or the annual allowance. These charges effectively ensure that such excessive contributions are not attractive from an investment perspective.

Furthermore, whilst the annual allowance and the lifetime allowance govern the maximum contributions which may be made to qualifying pension schemes during the year (without incurring a tax charge), the amount of gross contributions qualifying for tax relief is also limited to the greater of:

a) £3,600, or
b) The taxpayer's total 'earnings' for the tax year.

Since basic-rate tax relief at 20% is given at source on the contributions, the maximum net contribution qualifying for relief in 2011/12 is therefore the greater of:

a) £2,880, or
b) 80% of the taxpayer's total 'earnings' for the tax year.

This time, these limits **do** operate by reference to contributions actually made during the tax year!

In 2011/12, an individual with 'earnings' of £200,000 or more, who has not made any pension savings since 2007/8 (but has been a member of a registered pension scheme since then), and has existing pension funds not exceeding £1.6m, could theoretically obtain tax relief of up to £100,000 by making the maximum qualifying net pension contribution of £160,000 (i.e. 80% of their available annual allowance of £200,000).

51

They should, however, apply for 'fixed protection' from the lifetime allowance if this took the total value of their pension funds over £1.5m.

The 'Earnings' Problem

A major problem for many people is the fact that 'earnings' include only employment income and self-employed or partnership trading income. Many sources of income, including interest, dividends and most rental income, are not classed as earnings for pension purposes.

Furthermore, the current regime does not allow taxpayers to base pension contributions on their earnings in previous tax years. The current system is based on current year earnings only.

It may sometimes be important, therefore, to consider maximising pension contributions in the current tax year when a fall in 'earnings', as defined above, is anticipated. This might include those who:

- Form a limited company to take over a business or partnership.

- Give up employment to pursue another form of income which may not qualify as 'earnings' – e.g. rental income.

- Expect to benefit from significant tax reliefs next year (e.g. capital allowances).

Higher Rates of Relief

With the spectre of any restrictions on higher-rate tax relief banished (for the time being at least), personal pension contributions continue to attract relief at the investor's highest marginal rate of tax.

For those with income over £150,000, the tax relief on pension contributions will total 50%: 20% given at source and another 30% refunded via self-assessment.

But another group of individuals have the opportunity to obtain tax relief at up to 60% on their pension contributions.

This is due to the withdrawal of personal allowances for those with income over £100,000 which we examined in Chapter 1.

As explained in Chapter 1, the withdrawal of personal allowances will create an effective marginal rate of Income Tax of 60% on 'adjusted net income' between £100,000 and £114,950 (at 2011/12 rates).

As gross pension contributions are deducted in arriving at 'adjusted net income', this will make pension contributions more valuable to people in this marginal tax bracket.

For example, a person with taxable income of £110,000 for 2011/12 makes a personal pension contribution of £8,000. This is 'grossed up' by basic rate tax at 20% to make a gross contribution of £10,000. The gross contribution extends the taxpayer's basic rate band by £10,000, thus saving £2,000 (i.e. an extra £10,000 is taxed at 20% instead of 40%).

In addition, however, the gross contribution also reduces the taxpayer's 'adjusted net income' by £10,000, thus preserving an extra £5,000 of their personal allowance and saving a further £2,000 in Income Tax (£5,000 x 40%).

A net contribution of £8,000 therefore yields total Income Tax savings of £4,000, or £6,000 when we include the basic rate relief given at source. That's a total of 75% relief on the net contribution!

Pension Contribution Guidelines 2011/12

As explained at the beginning of this chapter, pensions are a form of investment and it is important to take professional advice before deciding whether or not to make pension contributions and how much to contribute.

Furthermore, as discussed earlier, whether you wish to use pensions as your preferred form of saving is very much a personal choice – they are not everyone's 'cup of tea'!

Here, however, I set out my quick guide to the tax considerations surrounding pension contributions made during 2011/12. The position is dependent on your current and future income and on your pattern of contributions over the previous three tax years.

In the headings given below 'Income' means total taxable income for 2011/12 before deducting any pension contributions. Once you have made sufficient contributions to put you in a different income bracket, however, you should switch to the guidance given for your new income bracket.

For example, if you have expected taxable income of £52,475 for 2011/12, you should start by looking at the second section below but, once you have made gross contributions of £10,000 (£8,000 net), you should switch to the first section.

Income under £42,475

As a basic rate taxpayer, you will only be able to obtain basic rate relief. You may wish to consider deferring pension contributions if you anticipate higher income levels in the future which will push you into the higher rate tax bracket.

If you are not already a member of a registered pension scheme, however, a small contribution to open up a scheme (with a scheme year ending in 2011/12) will give you almost £50,000 of extra unused annual allowance available for use until 2014/15.

Income from £42,475 to £100,000 or from £114,950 to £150,000

You will obtain higher rate tax relief as usual and may therefore wish to consider maximising your pension contributions.

The main exception to this will be where you anticipate a higher marginal rate of tax (50% or 60%) in the near future, in which case you might wish to defer some of your contributions.

Remember, however, that any unused annual allowance for 2008/9 will not be available to you again after 2011/12. (See also the 'Wealth Warning' below.)

Income from £100,000 to £114,950

As explained above, you will obtain tax relief at an effective rate of 60%.

This means that you should seriously consider making at least enough 'gross' pension contributions to reduce your 'adjusted net income' (see above) down to £100,000. It is probable that you will get very few chances (perhaps none) to obtain relief at such a high effective rate again.

Beyond that, you will be in the same position as other higher-rate taxpayers, as described above.

Income over £150,000

Since you will obtain tax relief at 50%, it is worth considering maximising your pension contributions within the available limits (the annual allowance, the lifetime allowance and your earnings level).

In particular, you may wish to make sufficient contributions to use up your annual allowance for 2011/12 and any unused annual allowance for 2008/9: your unused annual allowance for 2008/9 will simply go to waste if you do not utilise it this year.

Wealth Warning for all Higher-Rate Taxpayers

As discussed at the beginning of this chapter, the new Coalition Government appears to have moved away from the idea of an abolition of higher-rate tax relief for pension contributions.

However, the possibility of such a step at some point in the future, either by this Government or a later one, cannot be ruled out.

For this reason, it may make sense for all higher-rate taxpayers to maximise their pension contributions in the next few years, subject to the constraints of the annual allowance, the lifetime allowance, earnings levels, and, of course, available cash!

Chapter 5

Tax Return Tips

Tax Returns

Most higher-rate taxpayers and people in receipt of any gross, untaxed income will fall into the self-assessment system.

Under the self-assessment system, the taxpayer must complete and submit a tax return each year by:

- 31st October following the tax year for paper returns, or
- 31st January following the tax year for online returns.

If your return reaches HM Revenue & Customs by the above deadlines they will calculate the amount of tax you are due to pay. Frankly, however, I would not recommend relying on HM Revenue and Customs' calculations!

Tax Payments

The Income Tax due under the self-assessment system is basically the taxpayer's total tax liability for the year less any amounts already deducted at source or under PAYE and less any applicable tax credits (**not** Child Tax Credits or Working Tax Credits – despite their names, these are not part of the Income Tax system).

All Income Tax due under the self-assessment system, regardless of the source of the income or rate of tax applying, is payable as follows:

- A first instalment or 'payment on account' is due on 31st January during the tax year.
- A second payment on account is due on 31st July following the tax year.
- A balancing payment or, in some cases, a repayment, is due on 31st January following the tax year.

Each payment on account is usually equal to half of the previous tax year's self-assessment tax liability. However, payments on account need not be made when the previous year's self-assessment liability was either:

a) No more than £1,000, or
b) Less than 20% of the taxpayer's total tax liability for the year.

Hence, where a taxpayer's self-assessment liability for 2010/11 is no more than £1,000, no payments on account will be due on 31st January or 31st July 2012.

The £1,000 threshold referred to above was formerly set at £500 in respect of payments on account due up to 31st July 2009.

The Self-Assessment 'Double Whammy'

The system of payments on account under self-assessment, as described above, causes major cashflow problems whenever a taxpayer first receives a new source of income, or experiences a significant increase in any existing source of income outside the PAYE system.

Effectively, one and a half years' worth of tax on the new source, or the increase, falls due on 31st January following the tax year. Six months later, another half year's worth of tax becomes payable, meaning that two years' worth of tax must be paid within a six month period.

This is often the cause of major cashflow problems and it is imperative that anyone receiving a new source of income for the first time, or experiencing a significant increase in any income which is not within the PAYE system, makes appropriate provision for the tax arising.

Example

In April 2011, William buys an apartment block in a popular seaside resort. During 2011/12, this property yields rental profits of £20,000.

William's other income totals £80,000. Prior to 2011/12, all of his income was received under the PAYE system. Hence, on 31st January

2013, William has to pay additional Income Tax under the self-assessment system for the first time. On that date, he will have to pay a total of £12,000, made up of £8,000 tax due for 2011/12 (£20,000 x 40%) and his first payment on account for 2012/13 of £4,000 (half of £8,000).

Furthermore, William will also have to make a second payment on account of £4,000 in respect of 2012/13 on 31ˢᵗ July 2013. By this point, William has had to pay Income Tax equivalent to 80% of his first year's profits!

This position will now be even worse in some cases. If William's existing income had been £150,000 or more, he would have had to pay £15,000 on 31ˢᵗ January 2013 and £5,000 on 31ˢᵗ July 2013: totalling 100% of his first year's profits.

If William's existing income had been between £94,950 and £100,000, his tax bill on 31ˢᵗ January 2013 would have been £16,485. Add in a further £5,495 due on 31ˢᵗ July 2013 and this totals almost 110% of his first year's profits!

(It could even be up to 138% in other cases!)

What If Income Reduces?

Applications to reduce payments on account may be made when there are reasonable grounds to believe that the following year's self-assessment tax liability will be at a lower level.

Reduced payments on account may then be made based on the estimated self-assessment tax liability for the following year. If, however, it later transpires that the actual liability for the following year is greater than the reduced payments on account made by the taxpayer, interest will be charged on the difference.

Nevertheless, in certain circumstances, this provides scope to avoid the adverse cashflow impact of the payments on account system.

Example

Yvonne has a salary of £50,000 and also owns a small trading company. In 2011/12, Yvonne takes a dividend of £20,000 out of her company. This gives rise to a self-assessment tax liability of £5,000 due on 31ˢᵗ January 2013.

Normally, Yvonne would also have to make payments on account of £2,500 on 31ˢᵗ January and 31ˢᵗ July 2013. However, she decides to refrain from taking any dividends out of her company during 2012/13 and is therefore able to reduce her payments on account to nil.

As Yvonne does not take any dividends out of her company during 2012/13, she has no self-assessment tax liability to pay on 31ˢᵗ January 2014 and does not need to make any payments on account on 31ˢᵗ January or 31ˢᵗ July 2014.

In 2013/14, therefore, she will be able to take dividends again without having had to make any payments on account in respect of this income.

In other words, where a taxpayer can arrange to receive income bi-annually, they are able to avoid making any payments on account.

Self-Assessment and PAYE

Individuals with self-assessment tax liabilities not exceeding £2,000 who are also in employment or in receipt of a private pension may apply to have the tax collected through their PAYE codes for the following tax year.

This produces a considerable cashflow advantage, where relevant.

HM Revenue and Customs will only guarantee this treatment when you submit your online tax return by 30ᵗʰ December following the tax year or submit your paper tax return by 31ˢᵗ October. *(E.g. submit your online tax return for the year ending 5ᵗʰ April 2011 by 30ᵗʰ December 2011 to claim to have up to £2,000 collected through your PAYE coding for 2012/13.)*

Investment Income and PAYE

Wealth Warning

HM Revenue and Customs is now attempting to collect Income Tax on up to £10,000 of estimated annual investment income, including rental income, interest and dividends, through the PAYE system whenever possible (i.e. where the taxpayer also has employment income or private pensions).

This results in the tax on this income being paid on a 'current year' basis as it arises, just like the tax on salaries or private pensions. Even when HM Revenue and Customs get their estimates right, this accelerates the payment of tax on this income by an average of more than six months.

For a higher rate taxpayer with an overdraft, the resultant interest cost could be equivalent to around an extra 2.5% tax charge!

Furthermore, where HM Revenue and Customs overestimates the investment income, the excess tax paid will need to be reclaimed through the self-assessment system and interest will only run on the repayment from 31st January, almost nine months after the end of the tax year, or an average of almost sixteen months after payment of the excess tax.

(In fact, since January 2009 the rate of interest on overpaid tax has been zero, meaning that anyone who overpays tax is currently receiving no compensation at all!)

Worse still, where the taxpayer might otherwise have been able to apply to have up to £2,000 of tax collected through a later year's PAYE coding, as explained above, this approach by HM Revenue and Customs would result in tax payments being accelerated by two years!

HM Revenue and Customs dresses this approach up as being for 'your benefit' and 'to help you plan your finances'. Clearly, the Treasury has been infected by our politicians' fondness for spin!

The collection of tax on investment income through PAYE is **not** for your benefit, it is merely a way for the Government to accelerate the collection of tax. I would urge all readers who are in the PAYE system to check their coding notices and, if estimated investment income has been included, exercise your right to have this removed from your PAYE code. HM Revenue and Customs **must** comply with this request if you object to your PAYE code being used in this way and the instructions on how to do this are included on your PAYE coding notice.

Naturally, once investment income has been removed from your PAYE coding, you will need to ensure that you are able to pay the tax arising when it falls due under the self-assessment system. As explained above, this can be especially painful when the 'double-whammy' effect comes into play.

Nevertheless, the PAYE system is most certainly not the way to save up for your tax liabilities! Instead, I would generally recommend an ISA, a high-interest bearing deposit account (well, as high as you can find), or an offset mortgage.

New Sources of Untaxed Income

Strictly speaking, whenever you begin receiving untaxed income from a new source, you should advise HM Revenue & Customs by 5th October following the tax year in which it first arises. New sources of income for this purpose include:

- Self-employment trading income
- Partnership trading income
- UK rental income
- Interest received gross
- Foreign rental income
- Foreign interest (see Wealth Warning below)
- 'Large' foreign dividends (see Chapter 1)

In practice, though, as long as the taxpayer completes and submits a tax return by the usual deadline, includes the new source of income and pays the full amount of tax due on time, there are generally no penalties for failure to report most new sources of income by the 5th October deadline.

There are two important provisos that I need to make here, however.

Firstly, there are special rules for trading income which mean that, in reality, a far earlier deadline will actually apply in most cases. We will look at these rules shortly.

Secondly, if you are not already in the self-assessment system, you will find it extremely difficult to file your tax return if you have not already advised HM Revenue and Customs of your new source of income and obtained a Unique Taxpayer Reference ('UTR') number.

HM Revenue and Customs is now rejecting paper tax returns where they do not have a UTR for the taxpayer. Furthermore, filing online without a UTR is all but impossible!

If you are unable to file your tax return on time, you could be severely penalised and the fact that HM Revenue and Customs failed to issue you with a UTR in time will be no excuse if you did not advise them of your new source of income by the 5th October deadline. Hence, a deadline which was once merely theoretical has, in effect, sprouted some real teeth!

So, if you are not already in the self-assessment system, it is now vital to advise HM Revenue and Customs of your new source of income before the 5th October deadline. They will then need to issue you with a notice to complete a tax return and this will provide you with that essential UTR which you need to file your return.

If HM Revenue and Customs have still failed to issue you with a UTR by 31st October after the end of the relevant tax year, you will have an extended deadline for filing your tax return: three months from the date of issue of the notice to complete a tax return. The same extended deadline applies whether you file online or complete a paper tax return. (In fact, the extended deadline would also apply to a paper tax return where the notice to complete a tax return was issued after 31st July following the tax year.)

You will, however, still need to pay your tax on time and, if you are more than 30 days late (e.g. your payment does not reach HM Revenue and Customs by 1st March 2012 in the case of any tax due for 2010/11), an additional 5% surcharge will be added.

Again, it is difficult to pay HM Revenue and Customs without a UTR: they have been known to return payments under these circumstances – and then charge penalties and interest for late payment!

In summary, therefore, if you are not already in the self-assessment system and have a new source of income to report (or a capital gain – see Chapter 12), I would recommend that you advise HM Revenue and Customs as soon as possible.

For small amounts of investment income, HM Revenue and Customs may choose to tax you through the PAYE system. As explained above, this has some inherent cashflow disadvantages, so you may prefer not to accept this approach. For very small amounts, however, you may find it more convenient and you will still have fulfilled your obligations under the tax system.

There is just one potential drawback to advising HM Revenue and Customs of your new source of income too early: they may issue you with a notice to complete a tax return for the wrong year!

Once you have been issued with a notice to complete a tax return, you have an obligation to complete it, even if you have no sources of untaxed income for the year.

Generally speaking, therefore, my advice to anyone not yet in the self-assessment system is to advise HM Revenue and Customs of a new source of untaxed income on 6th April (the day after the tax year in which the new source first arises), or as soon as possible thereafter. This will hopefully prevent them from getting confused about which tax year is involved but still give them enough time to issue you with a UTR.

Except, that is, for trading income: the day after the end of the tax year should be good enough for most new sources of income, but the position for trading income is different.

New Traders

An individual who commences trading as a sole trader or as a partner in a trading partnership must register with HM Revenue and Customs for Class 2 National Insurance within three months of the end of the calendar month in which trading commences. Failure to register on time carries a penalty of £100.

Professions and vocations carried out on a self-employed basis, or through a partnership, are treated as trading for almost all tax purposes, including this one.

Wealth Warning: Foreign Interest

The Government has proposed to introduce a new requirement for UK residents to advise HM Revenue and Customs immediately if they open any form of account with a bank or other deposit-taking institution based in a 'tax haven'. Penalties of up to 100% of the tax due on interest earned on the account may be applied if the taxpayer fails to comply.

Personal Pension Payments Made Directly by Employers

Employers making personal pension payments on behalf of their employees may choose to either operate the 'net pay arrangements' or to operate basic rate tax relief at source.

It is important to understand which method is being operated.

Under the net pay arrangements, full tax relief is already given via the PAYE system and the employee need not make any further claim in their tax return. Where only basic rate tax relief is given at source, however, the employee needs to ensure that they claim any higher rate tax relief due via their tax return.

Chapter 6

Giving to Charity: How to Save Even More Tax

Gift Aid Donations

There are no minimum or maximum limits on donations to charity made under Gift Aid and, from the donor's point of view, there are no particular record keeping requirements. Having said that, however, in the event of an enquiry you will need to be able to prove that you made any donations for which you have claimed tax relief.

There is also the practical matter of remembering the Gift Aid donations which you have made when the time comes to complete your tax return. I suspect that a great many people fail to claim all of the relief which they are due simply because they failed to keep a record of the donations made during the year.

Hence, whilst there are no particular record-keeping requirements for Gift Aid donations, I would recommend that some type of record is kept.

Gift Aid donations are made net of basic rate tax and effectively attract relief at the taxpayer's top rate of Income Tax, often 40% or 50%. For every £10 which a taxpayer donates to charity by means of Gift Aid, a sum of £2.50 (20/80ths) will be deemed to have been deducted from their payment in respect of basic-rate tax. The charity is able to recover this sum from the Government.

A taxpayer who has made a £10 donation under Gift Aid is effectively treated as having made a tax-deductible gross donation of £12.50, on which basic rate tax relief has already been given.

The effect of this depends on the donor's marginal rate of Income Tax. We will look at the position for those whose marginal Income Tax rate is now 50% or 60% a little later (see under 'Further Benefits' below).

Higher Rate Taxpayers

For a higher-rate taxpayer, the total tax relief generated by a net donation of £10 made during 2011/12 will be £5.00 (£12.50 at 40%).

Of this, however, £2.50 is deemed to have been received already, by way of a reduction in the donation itself, so that the net saving actually achieved is £2.50, or 25% of the amount of the donation.

Hence, in this rather long-winded fashion, a £10 Gift Aid donation actually costs a higher rate taxpayer £7.50. The Government pays out £5.00 in total and the charity receives a total of £12.50.

Basic Rate Taxpayers

For a basic rate taxpayer, the tax relief generated by the deemed donation of £12.50 is £2.50 – the same amount of relief that is deemed to have already been given at source. In other words, whilst Gift Aid still benefits the charity to which they have made the donation, it makes absolutely no difference to the basic rate taxpayer.

Starting Rate and Non-Taxpayers

By making a net payment of £10 under Gift Aid, the taxpayer is effectively guaranteeing to pay Income Tax of at least £2.50.

Hence, whilst Gift Aid is beneficial to higher rate taxpayers, and of no direct consequence to basic rate taxpayers, it can prove to be a costly mistake for non-taxpayers.

In essence, if your tax bill ultimately proves to be less than the basic rate tax deemed to have been 'deducted' from your donation, you will have to pay the difference over to HM Revenue & Customs.

Wealth Warning

As stated above, there is no statutory maximum amount of Gift Aid donations which a taxpayer may make in any tax year. However, it is important to remember that if the total amount of tax deemed to be deducted from the donations exceeds the taxpayer's total tax liability for the year, they will need to pay over the difference to HM Revenue and Customs.

Carrying Donations Back to the Previous Year

Donations made after the end of the tax year but before the earlier of:

i)   the following 31st January, or
ii) the date on which your tax return for the year is submitted,

may be carried back for relief in the previous tax year.

Specific donations must be chosen for the carry back; it is not possible to carry back part of a donation or a simple numeric amount. It is worth bearing this in mind when making donations and perhaps splitting large donations into smaller amounts to assist in subsequent planning.

The legislation also appears to require that the tax return incorporating the claim for gift aid donations carried back from the following year must be submitted by 31st January (i.e. by the online filing deadline), although I have never seen this point taken in practice.

The carry back facility is highly beneficial to any charitable taxpayers whose income level has dropped from one tax year to the next, such that they are no longer a higher rate taxpayer.

Example

Bob makes a gift aid donation of £8,000 on 18th January 2012.

Bob's taxable income for 2010/11 was £60,000, making him a higher rate taxpayer for that year.

Bob knows that his taxable income for 2011/12 will be no more than £20,000 at the most, meaning that he will only be a basic rate taxpayer for the current year.

As things stand, therefore, Bob will receive no additional tax relief for his donation in January 2012.

Fortunately, however, Bob's accountants, the 'Boomtown Accounting Co.', submit his 2011 tax return online on 25th January 2012 and they are therefore able to make a claim for him to carry his Gift Aid donation back to 2010/11 for relief in that year.

This claim will save Bob £2,000 in Income Tax on 31st January 2012.

It can readily be seen that the ability to claim relief in the previous tax year can be used to almost eliminate the usual delay in obtaining full, higher-rate, Income Tax relief on Gift Aid donations. A further cashflow advantage will also often arise from the fact that the self-assessment instalment payments for the next tax year will also be reduced.

This provides a powerful incentive to delay the submission of online tax returns until shortly before the 31st January deadline whenever there is a possibility of Gift Aid donations being made. (But remember that paper tax returns must be submitted by 31st October following the tax year.)

Where an individual is paying higher rate tax in both the current and previous tax years, the carry back of Gift Aid donations made between 6th April and the date of submission of their previous year's tax return will still generate a cashflow saving, even if not an absolute one.

Carry back of Gift Aid donations should also be considered where the taxpayer is at risk of being a non-taxpayer in the current tax year.

A carry back should not be done, however, when the taxpayer was a basic rate, starting rate or non-taxpayer last year, but may be a higher rate taxpayer this year.

Furthermore, for those expecting income over £100,000 in 2011/12, there will be some situations where a carry back of Gift Aid donations made after 5th April 2011 would be disadvantageous.

On the other hand, there may also be some situations where carrying back a small Gift Aid donation could be incredibly beneficial – saving you tens of thousands of pounds!

Further Benefits

In Chapter 1 we looked at the effective marginal rate of Income Tax of 60% on income from £100,000 to £114,950, as well as the 'super tax' rate of 50% on income over £150,000.

The grossed up amount of any Gift Aid donations effectively reduces the donor's income for all Income Tax purposes.

This means that individuals with income between £100,000 and £114,950 in 2011/12 will obtain effective relief at 60% on their gross Gift Aid donations. Looked at another way, a net donation of £10 will produce total tax relief of £7.50, of which £2.50 is given at source and £5 is received through the self-assessment system.

For those with income over £150,000 in 2011/12, a net donation of £10 will produce total tax relief of £6.25, of which £2.50 is given at source and £3.75 is received through the self-assessment system.

Anyone anticipating income falling into either of these bands in 2011/12 should therefore not generally carry back any donations made in 2011/12 to 2010/11 unless they were suffering the same marginal tax rate, or even higher, in the earlier year.

Conversely, of course, anyone who had income falling into either of these bands in 2010/11, but not in 2011/12, could benefit greatly from carrying back their Gift Aid donations.

Anyone anticipating income falling into either of these high tax bands in 2012/13, but not in 2011/12, may also wish to consider deferring any Gift Aid donations until after 5th April 2012.

Wealth Warning

The Government is considering revising the Gift Aid regime to move the benefit of higher rate tax relief from the donor to the recipient charity. Whether this will actually happen and, if so, when, is unclear. Nevertheless, if such a change does take place, higher rate taxpayers will lose the benefit of this relief in the future.

Although, as discussed above, there may be cases where higher rate taxpayers could benefit by deferring Gift Aid donations until after 5th April 2012, this does carry a degree of risk, as it will only be beneficial if the current regime continues.

Gift Aid and Pension Contributions

Gift Aid donations carried back to 2010/11 can be used to reduce an individual's adjusted income for that year below the £130,000 or £150,000 threshold for the purposes of the 'anti-forestalling' charge on pension contributions.

Where Gift Aid donations are carried back, they are treated as if they had been made in the previous year for all Income Tax purposes.

Hence, any Gift Aid donations made this year, but carried back to 2010/11, will reduce the taxpayer's adjusted income for that year for the purposes of the 'anti-forestalling' charge on pension contributions.

In some cases, this could enable an individual who made large pension contributions in 2010/11 to retain higher rate tax relief, thus saving an amount of tax equal to 25% of their net contributions (see Chapter 4).

(See the Taxcafe.co.uk guide *'How to Save Tax 2010/11'* for full details of the 'anti-forestalling' charge. Email team@taxcafe.co.uk for a complimentary copy if required.)

Example

Rose, a prominent local businesswoman and well-known advocate of lower taxation, had gross income of £145,000 in both 2008/9 and 2009/10. In both of those years, she also made gross pension contributions of £20,000, meaning that her adjusted income for the purposes of the 'anti-forestalling' charge was £125,000 for each year – under the £130,000 threshold. In 2010/11, Rose had gross income of £150,499. She again made a gross pension contribution of £20,000, but this only brought her adjusted income down to £130,499 – still over the £130,000 threshold.

Later in 2010/11, Rose made a further net pension contribution of £68,800 (or £86,000 gross). As things stand, she will be subject to the 'anti-forestalling' charge and will lose her higher-rate tax relief on this larger contribution.

On 4th January 2012, however, Rose makes a net donation of £400 to TIBA (the Tax Inspectors' Benevolent Association – a registered charity) under gift aid. TIBA writes to Rose, confirming that her donation is eligible under the gift aid scheme and therefore treated as a gross donation of £500. TIBA also expresses some surprise at her generosity given her well known views on tax. "No, no, that's OK", replies Rose, "I'm happy to contribute. I know you've all just got a job to do."

What TIBA doesn't realise is that, by carrying her gift aid donation back to 2010/11, Rose is able to reduce her adjusted income for that year, for the purposes of the 'anti-forestalling' charge, down to £129,999 and thus escape the charge. This effectively restores her higher-rate tax relief on her additional gross pension contribution of £86,000.

Her £400 donation to TIBA therefore saves Rose a total of £17,300 in higher rate Income Tax. No wonder she was happy to contribute!

There are anti-avoidance provisions designed to prevent individuals like Rose from using 'schemes' to bring their adjusted income under £130,000 in order to avoid the anti-forestalling charge.

It seems unlikely, however, that a gift aid donation to a completely unconnected charity could be construed as a 'scheme'. In practice, though, you might want to choose a less unusual charity for your donation.

Gift Aid on Admissions to Museums, Etc.

Certain heritage and conservation charities can treat admission fees to museums, art galleries, zoos, etc, as a Gift Aid donation, thus enabling them to receive an additional 25% from the Government. However, the charities have to charge a 10% supplement on admission fees in order for them to be eligible for Gift Aid.

For higher rate taxpayers, it remains beneficial to pay the additional 10% supplement, as this will still produce an overall saving of 17.5%.

For example, you could pay £10 to enter a museum, or £11 as a Gift Aid donation which also gives you right of entry. After higher rate tax relief, however, your £11 donation will cost you only £8.25, or 17.5% less than the normal admission fee.

This saving increases to 31.25% for those with total income over £150,000 and to 45% for those suffering the 60% marginal tax rate.

As with all other Gift Aid donations, I would recommend getting a receipt. Not because you are required to, but because it's the only way that you'll ever remember all these donations when you're filling in your next tax return!

Paying the supplement will always benefit the charity, but for anyone other than a higher rate taxpayer, this will come at a cost. For non-taxpayers, there will be an additional 'hidden' cost in addition to the 10% supplement on the entry fee.

Wealth Warning

Non-higher rate taxpayers beware: some charitable organisations do their utmost to hide the fact that they are charging you the 10% supplement in order to ensure that your admission fee is treated as a Gift Aid donation. Be careful to check the true position before paying your entry fee. You may be happy to make the extra 10% donation but you ought to be given a choice.

European Charities

Prior to 6th April 2010 (but possibly earlier – see below), Gift Aid could only apply to payments to UK charities.

However, following a decision at the European Court of Justice, the UK has now been forced to revise its treatment of charities based elsewhere in the European Economic Area.

Payments under Gift Aid may therefore now be made to charities located anywhere in the European Union or in Iceland or Norway.

Furthermore, as the change arises due to a decision under European law (which takes precedence over UK law), HM Revenue and Customs will be required to consider claims in respect of charitable payments made between 27th January 2009 (the date of the decision) and 5th April 2010 on a 'case by case' basis.

English case law principles will be used to determine whether any organisation qualifies as a charity.

Chapter 7

Tax Tips for Business Owners & Landlords

In this chapter, we will explore some of the tax planning issues common to all types of business, as well as some of the issues specific to unincorporated businesses (sole traders and partnerships). Further issues specific to people with their own companies will be covered in the next chapter.

Generally, for most tax reliefs applying to businesses, it is the business's own accounting period and year end date which is the critical deadline. There are, however, a few matters where the end of the tax year provides the critical deadline date.

'Family Allowances'

Those with a spouse, partner or other family member working in their business may wish to maximise the use of personal allowances by ensuring that these employees receive sufficient salary or wages each tax year to utilise their personal allowances (generally £7,475 for 2011/12, but see Appendix A for further details).

Note, however, that payments in excess of the National Insurance primary threshold (£7,225 for 2011/12) made to employees aged 16 or over, but below state retirement age, will be subject to Class 1 National Insurance at 12%.

All payments to employees aged 16 or more in excess of the secondary threshold (£7,075 for 2011/12) will be subject to employer's National Insurance at 13.8%.

In both cases, the National Insurance should only be due on the amount paid in excess of the threshold (provided you time the payments correctly).

Most payments in excess of £7,225 will therefore give rise to a total National Insurance cost of 25.8% of the excess (plus a further £20.70 in employer's National Insurance).

In some cases, it may therefore make sense to limit any salary payments to family members for 2011/12 to a maximum of £7,075 or £7,225, rather than the full amount of the personal allowance.

However, where the employer is a higher rate taxpayer sole trader, or a partnership comprised predominantly of higher rate taxpayer individuals, a salary equal to the full personal allowance will often remain beneficial overall for tax purposes.

The total National Insurance cost of the additional salary over the two earnings thresholds will be £85.20, including employer's National Insurance of £55.20.

However, the total tax relief received by the higher rate taxpayer employer on the extra £400 salary over the secondary threshold will be £191.18 (£400 + £55.20 = £455.20 x 42%), thus producing an overall net saving of £105.98 (£191.18 - £85.20).

Naturally, the saving will be even greater for employers paying marginal Income Tax rates of 50% or 60%.

Any salary payments should, of course:

- Only be considered when justified by the amount of effort put into the business by the intended recipient,

- Actually be paid to the employee, and

- Be reported to HM Revenue & Customs as required under the PAYE system (even if no Income Tax or National Insurance is actually due).

Where justified, salary payments to family members should attract tax relief in the employer's business.

A further benefit of these payments is the fact that, provided payments exceed the level of £102 per week, the recipient will be entitled to state benefits, including a state pension on reaching state retirement age.

PAYE and National Insurance

When making small salary payments, it is important to beware of the weekly or monthly payment thresholds which usually apply for PAYE and National Insurance purposes.

Each employer has to operate PAYE by reference to 'pay periods'. A 'pay period' will usually be either a week or a month, depending on how the employer operates their payroll. Although it is possible to use other pay periods, it can be difficult to administer them in practice (partly because the necessary payroll software is not always available). Furthermore, when paying family members, it is likely that the same pay periods will be used as for other employees – and this will nearly always be weekly or monthly.

For Income Tax purposes, the personal allowance and basic rate tax band are divided over all of the pay periods in the tax year. When a payment is made to an employee, only the cumulative proportion for the tax year to date can be taken into account.

Still, when it comes to Income Tax, it does all 'come out in the wash' and if the pay period system results in an overpayment, the excess can always be reclaimed subsequently: when another salary payment is made, through the self-assessment system, or by way of a repayment claim.

Sadly, National Insurance does not operate in the same way. Unlike Income Tax, there is generally no scope for reclaiming any excess National Insurance payments when the final total pay for the tax year is known.

For most employees (except company directors – see Chapter 8), any payment in excess of the secondary threshold for the pay period will attract employer's secondary National Insurance at 13.8% and any payment in excess of the primary threshold for the pay period will also attract a further 12% in employee's primary National Insurance.

That's a total cost of up to 25.8% which **cannot** be recovered!

For 2011/12, the secondary threshold is £136 for weekly pay periods or £589 for monthly pay periods and the primary threshold is £139 for weekly pay periods or £602 for monthly pay periods. Hence, when paying a small salary to a family member, it will usually be necessary to pay them on a regular basis over the course of the tax year, and not in irregular lump sums, in order to avoid any unwanted National Insurance liabilities.

Higher Salaries for Family Members

When employing your spouse, partner or other family members in a business, it may be worth considering whether to pay them sufficient salary to utilise their basic rate tax band.

However, it must be borne in mind that payments in excess of the primary threshold will generally be subject to both employee's and employer's National Insurance Contributions.

The total National Insurance cost on most salary payments in excess of the primary threshold in 2011/12 will be 25.8%.

Nevertheless, small overall tax savings can sometimes still be achieved where the employer is a higher rate taxpayer.

More significant savings will be achieved where the employer is paying marginal rates of combined Income Tax and National Insurance of 52% or 62% on their trading profits (see Chapter 1).

Year-End Planning

As explained above, the critical deadline for most year-end planning is the business's own accounting date. Most businesses are generally free to choose their own accounting date, although landlords must usually pay tax based on their rental profits for the year ending 5th April unless they are using a company.

As the business's accounting year end approaches, some steps may be taken to reduce the amount of taxable profit for the year, including the following:

- Purchasing assets eligible for capital allowances
- Payment of bonuses to employees
- Undertaking necessary repairs and maintenance work

It is always worth bearing in mind that business expenditure is allowable when incurred, not when it is paid for.

Example

Tom and Barbara run a small market gardening business. They have a 31st March accounting date for tax purposes. In March 2012 they have some repairs done to their barn roof. They do not receive an invoice for the work until May 2012 and do not pay it until July 2012. Despite not having to pay for this cost until July 2012, Tom and Barbara are entitled to claim it in their accounts for the year ended 31st March 2012.

Accelerate or Defer

The year-end planning described above is designed to defer taxable income until the following year. As explained in Chapter 2, it is usually preferable to defer taxable income whenever legitimately possible. However, as also detailed in Chapter 2, there are some people who may be better off accelerating their taxable income.

In this respect, it is important for sole traders and business partnerships to note that, where your current accounting period ends on or before 5th April 2012, the profits arising will usually be wholly taxable in 2011/12, with the profits of your next accounting period similarly also usually being fully taxable in 2012/13.

The tables set out at the end of Chapter 2 can thus be used to determine whether you are in the usual position that it is better to defer income as far as legitimately possible, or in one of the situations where it is better to accelerate income where legitimately possible – or at least to refrain from deferring it.

For those whose current accounting period ends after 5th April 2012, the profits arising will usually be wholly taxable in 2012/13. In these cases, the decision whether to defer or accelerate income will need to be based on a comparison of your likely marginal tax rates for 2012/13 and 2013/14. The forecasts set out in Chapter 2 and Appendices A and B may be of some assistance in this regard, but I would also add that there are rumours that the 50% 'super tax' rate may be abolished for 2013/14 onwards.

Where it does appear preferable to accelerate income, or defer expenditure, so that more profit falls into your current accounting period, some of the measures you might consider include:

- Completing sales earlier
- Deferring repairs and maintenance work
- Deferring payment of employee's bonuses
- Deferring purchases of assets eligible for capital allowances

Another option in some cases might be to change your accounting date, so that more profits fall into 2011/12. However, this will generally only be worthwhile where you expect lower profits in the near future, such as people close to retirement, for example.

Small Business Taxation Review

The taxation of small businesses is currently under review and a report on potential future changes is expected before the 2012 Budget. This means we may see draft proposals for a radical reform of small business taxation as early as next Spring, with a possible implementation date in 2013 or 2014.

One of the areas most likely to be targeted is couples and families operating businesses together through partnerships or companies (where previous Government attempts to impose 'income-shifting' legislation have so far failed: but the battle is not over yet!)

Other issues under consideration may include the boundary between employment and self-employment (and a possible replacement for the infamous 'IR35' legislation) and measures to remove the distortions to the tax system created by National Insurance (the Government is also consulting on the possibility of integrating the operation of Income Tax and National Insurance).

One idea being 'kicked around' is the possibility of a new (and perhaps compulsory) type of business entity to replace the small private company. HM Revenue and Customs would dearly love to see everyone taxed at the same rates as employees (who pay more tax than anyone else) and this may be its chance.

The 'status quo' may be the best that we can all hope for!

Chapter 8

Tax Tips for Company Owners

Corporation Tax Rates

In his second Budget on 23rd March 2011, Chancellor George Osborne announced a further reduction in the main rate of Corporation Tax in addition to the reductions in both the main rate and the small profits rate announced last year.

As a result, the main rate of Corporation Tax for large companies with annual profits in excess of £1.5m is now 26% - reduced from the previous rate of 28% with effect from 1st April 2011. This rate will be further reduced by 1% on 1st April each year from 2012 to 2014 so that it falls to just 23% by the end of this period.

On 1st April 2011 the 'small profits rate' applying to companies with annual profits of no more than £300,000 was reduced from 21% to 20%. This reduction applies instead of the old Labour Government's planned increase to 22% and thus represents a 2% saving compared with previous expectations.

For companies with annual profits between £300,000 and £1.5m, there is an effective marginal rate of Corporation Tax, which is currently 27.5%. The following table sets out the effective Corporation Tax rates for the period from 1st April 2008 to 31st March 2015:

Company Profit Band:	2008/9 to 2010/11	2011/12	2012/13	2013/14	2014/15
Up to £300,000	21%	20%	20%	20%	20%
£300,000 to £1.5m	29.75%	27.5%	26.25%	25%	23.75%
Over £1.5m	28%	26%	25%	24%	23%

The total Corporation Tax payable during this period at various levels of annual profit will be as follows:

Company Profits:	2008/9 to 2010/11	2011/12	2012/13	2013/14	2014/15
£50,000	£10,500	£10,000	£10,000	£10,000	£10,000
£100,000	£21,000	£20,000	£20,000	£20,000	£20,000
£300,000	£63,000	£60,000	£60,000	£60,000	£60,000
£500,000	£122,500	£115,000	£112,500	£110,000	£107,500
£1,000,000	£271,250	£252,500	£243,750	£235,000	£226,250

As we can see, all companies benefit from the Corporation Tax rate reductions taking place in 2011. Medium-sized and large companies will then continue to benefit from the further reductions in the main Corporation Tax rate taking place between 2012 and 2014.

All of the figures in the above tables are based on a single company with no associated companies.

Should Small Companies Accelerate Taxable Income?

Or, to put it another way, should they refrain from the usual tax planning measures designed to defer taxable income?

For companies with taxable profits around the £300,000 threshold, it remains worth bringing forward taxable profits whenever legitimately possible when the current year's profits lie below £300,000 and next year's profits are expected to exceed that level.

This will save Corporation Tax at between 7.5% and 8.75% for accounting periods ending during 2011/12, reducing the tax bill on the accelerated income by around 27% to 29%, which more than compensates for accelerating the tax liability by a year.

The amount saved by following this strategy may have reduced over the last few years, but it still remains a highly valid tax planning point.

Another good reason to accelerate income might be to provide sufficient distributable profits to support a dividend payment to shareholders on or before 5th April 2012. This point is discussed further below.

Using Your Own Personal Allowance

Company owners should consider whether they are taking sufficient salary out of their company to fully utilise the secondary National Insurance earnings threshold (£7,075 for 2011/12).

Whether it is worth increasing your own salary by a further £400 to fully utilise your personal allowance depends on a number of factors, including whether you have any other taxable income during the year.

This is a complex issue which is covered in detail in the Taxcafe.co.uk guide *'Salary versus Dividends'*.

However, for company owners with no other taxable income during 2011/12, it will generally be worth increasing your own salary up to the £7,225 primary National Insurance threshold in most cases. If your company has annual profits in excess of £307,530 before paying your salary, a further small increase to the level of the personal allowance (£7,475 for 2011/12) will also usually be worthwhile.

For directors, National Insurance is calculated on a cumulative basis. This means that the earnings thresholds are applied on an annual basis and not by reference to pay periods. A director may therefore be safely paid their salary in a lump sum without creating excess National Insurance liabilities.

Note that companies may choose to initially calculate National Insurance on directors' salaries in the same way as for other employees but an adjustment to the cumulative basis will be made at the end of the tax year.

Using the Basic Rate Tax Band – Dividends

Company owners should also consider whether to take sufficient dividends out of their company during the tax year to ensure that they fully utilise their basic rate tax band (£35,000 for 2011/12).

The 10% tax credit attaching to all dividends paid by a UK company is deemed to settle any Income Tax liability on the part of the recipient individual provided that they are not a higher rate taxpayer.

Hence, in the absence of any other income, an individual could receive dividends of £38,227* during 2011/12 and have no further Income Tax liability.

(* £38,227 plus the attached tax credit of $1/9^{th}$ equals £42,475, which is the total of the personal allowance and the basic rate tax band for 2011/12.)

If paying yourself a salary of £7,225, your maximum tax-free dividend becomes £31,725 and, with a salary of £7,475, it is £31,500.

However, dividends do not attract Corporation Tax relief and nor do they rank as relevant earnings for pension contribution purposes.

As a consequence of these and many other factors, it is sometimes worth considering whether to pay yourself a higher salary or a bonus instead (see the Taxcafe.co.uk guide *'Salary versus Dividends'* for a detailed analysis).

Where the company has insufficient funds to pay the necessary dividend, it could be declared, but left unpaid and owing to the intended recipient, until such time as the funds may sensibly be withdrawn from the company. HM Revenue and Customs may challenge the validity of unpaid dividends in these circumstances, although the legal basis for this stance is not clear.

Dividends may not, however, be declared where the company has insufficient distributable profits to cover them. Companies are required to have a set of accounts available which demonstrate that there are sufficient distributable profits to cover any dividend before it is declared.

Using Dividends to Avoid 'Super Tax'

As explained in Chapter 1, those with income over £150,000 are now subject to a 'super tax' rate of 50% on most income and an effective rate of 36.1% on dividend income.

Company owners whose personal income is currently less than £150,000, but who anticipate personal income over £150,000 next year, may therefore wish to consider paying themselves larger dividends on or before 5th April 2012.

It may also be preferable to take a larger dividend in 2011/12 instead of dividend income in 2012/13 which might be expected to fall into the marginal rate band from £100,000 to £116,210 (see Chapter 2 and Appendix A).

Conversely, it will generally be wise to avoid taking dividend income in 2011/12 which would fall into the marginal rate band from £100,000 to £114,950 this year (see Chapter 1).

Dividends Paid to Spouses, Partners and Other Family Members

Tax savings may also be generated by paying dividends to a spouse, partner or other family member up to the amount of their basic rate tax band.

This well-established tax planning strategy has, however, been under attack in recent years and may also be subject to further restrictions in the future.

Company owners planning to follow this strategy should therefore seek professional advice.

Chapter 9

Obtaining Tax Relief at More Than Your Marginal Tax Rate

Due to a quirk in the Income Tax system, it is sometimes possible to obtain tax relief at an effective rate which is higher than your marginal tax rate. Where this opportunity exists, it can be used to make even greater tax savings.

Example

In the tax year 2011/12, Morgan receives an annual salary of £42,475 plus dividends of £1,000.

Her Income Tax liability for the year is thus as follows:

Salary:	£42,475
Less: Personal Allowance:	£7,475

Total 'Other' Taxable Income	£35,000
Income Tax thereon @ 20%:	£7,000
Dividends Received:	£1,000
Plus Tax Credit (1/9th)	£111

Total	£1,111
Income Tax @ 32.5% less tax credit: £361 - £111	£250
Total Tax Due for 2011/12	£7,250

However, on 3rd April 2012, Morgan makes a pension contribution of £800 (net). This is equivalent to a gross contribution of £1,000 and the effect of this is to 'extend' her basic rate tax band by £1,000.

This 'extension' operates in addition to the tax relief of £200 already given at source and, as we will see, results in further tax savings.

Let's take a look at how this affects her Income Tax liability for the year:

Salary:	£42,475
Income Tax thereon (as before)	£7,000
Dividends Received:	£1,000
Plus Tax Credit (1/9th)	£111

Total	£1,111
Income Tax thereon:	
£1,000 @ 10%	£100
(extension to basic rate band)	
£111 @ 32.5% (the 'dividend rate')	£36

	£136
Less: Tax Credit	£111

Tax Payable on Dividend	£25
Total Tax Due for 2011/12	£7,025

As we can see, in addition to the £200 of tax relief given at source on her pension contribution, Morgan has also saved a further £225, making a total saving of £425, or 42.5% of her gross pension contribution (equivalent to over 53% of her net cash contribution of £800!)

From this example, we can now see that your marginal tax rate is not necessarily the limit to the rate of tax relief available under the right circumstances!

Reducing Payments on Account

It is also worth bearing in mind that any reduction in this year's Income Tax liability will also reduce the payments on account due under the self-assessment system (see Chapter 5).

As the first payment on account in respect of next year's tax is due at the same time as the balancing payment in respect of this year's tax, every £1 of tax saved actually produces a cashflow saving of £1.50.

In cashflow terms, a 40% saving becomes 60%, a 50% saving becomes 75% and a 60% saving would become 90%!

Chapter 10

The Pros & Cons of Company Cars

The term 'company car' applies to any car provided to an employee, even when the employer is not a company. In the specific case of companies, however, it is also possible for the company owner themselves to have a company car.

The annual chargeable benefit in kind on company cars for Income Tax and National Insurance purposes is based on the car's CO_2 emissions.

For most cars, the benefit in kind ranges from 15% to 35% of the car's original list price when new, depending on the car's CO_2 emissions level. Prior to 2011/12, the list price was capped at a maximum of £80,000 for this purpose, but this limit was abolished from 6th April 2011.

The benefit in kind charge starts at 15% for cars meeting a defined emissions level and then rises in steps of 1% for each 5g/km by which the car's CO_2 emissions exceed this level until reaching the maximum charge of 35%.

The car's emissions level for these purposes is rounded down to the nearest 5g/km. Hence, for example, a car with CO_2 emissions of 154.9g/km is treated as if it had emissions of 150g/km.

Diesel cars are subject to a 3% supplement but the maximum taxable benefit in kind remains 35%. The benefit in kind charge on most diesels therefore ranges from 18% to 35%.

On 6th April 2011, the company car regime was tightened yet again with a further reduction of 5g/km in the emissions level eligible for the lower benefit in kind charge of 15% to its current level of 125g/km. (In effect, due to the rounding down described above, this means cars with emissions of under 130g/km.)

The emissions levels used to determine company car benefits in kind will be further tightened over the next two years.

In 2012/13, there will be a more wide-ranging reform, with the introduction of further CO_2 emissions bands extending down to a new lower benefit in kind charge of 10% for cars with an emissions level of under 100g/km.

At this point, petrol cars with emissions between 120g/km and 124.99g/km will be subject to a benefit in kind charge of 15%.

The 3% supplement for diesel cars will continue to apply.

In 2013/14, the emissions levels will again be reduced by a further 5g/km, so that only cars with an emissions level of under 95g/km will be eligible for the new lower rate of 10%.

Practical Implications

The practical impact of this is that the benefit in kind charge on most company cars increased by a percentage point on 6th April 2011 and will do so again in each of the next two years.

For example, a car which had a benefit in kind charge of 19% in 2010/11 will have a benefit in kind charge of 20% in 2011/12, 21% in 2012/13 and 22% in 2013/14.

The benefit in kind for 2010/11 on such a car, which had an original list price when new of £20,000, would have been £3,800. This year, the benefit in kind charge on the same car will be £4,000 and it will increase to £4,400 by 2013/14. For a higher rate taxpayer this would produce an Income Tax cost of £1,520 in 2010/11 and £1,600 in 2011/12, increasing to £1,760 by 2013/14.

Furthermore, the employer must also pay Class 1A National Insurance on this benefit at the rate of 13.8% (12.8% prior to 2011/12). The Class 1A charge on the car described above would therefore have been £486 last year, £552 this year, and will increase to £607 by 2013/14.

These tax costs must be weighed against the fact that employers are able to claim the full cost of running and financing a company car plus capital allowances.

On the other hand, where any employee (including a company director) uses a privately owned car for business purposes, the employer may pay a mileage allowance of up to 45 pence per mile on the first 10,000 miles of business travel in each tax year (40 pence per mile prior to 2011/12).

This mileage allowance is tax-free in the employee's hands but may still be claimed as a business expense in the employer's accounts.

This tax-free mileage rate drops to 25 pence per mile after the first 10,000 business miles driven in each tax year.

An additional tax-free allowance of 5 pence per business mile may be claimed by the driver where a second employee (of the same business) travels as a passenger in their car.

Company owners with their own company cars may therefore wish to consider whether they might be better off owning their cars privately.

All employers should regularly review whether their employees' car schemes are still tax efficient.

Considerable savings may be possible in many cases and can often be shared between the employer and the employees.

In general terms, a company car remains worthwhile when private mileage is high but business mileage is low.

Conversely, owning the car privately generally tends to be more beneficial when private mileage is low and business mileage is high.

I know it sounds like I've got this back to front, but that really is the way that it works out. Pure 'perk' cars are often beneficial but the hard-working salesperson who really needs their company car may be better off using their own car for business!

Wealth Warning

When an employee uses their own private car for business purposes, they must ensure that their insurance policy covers them for business use.

Employers are also required to check that any car used for business purposes is insured for business use and is roadworthy (checking that it has a current M.O.T. would be advisable at the very least).

It is also important to ensure that the vehicle is taxed and the driver holds a full driving licence.

Low CO2-Emission Cars

In 2010/11 and 2011/12, the annual benefit in kind charge on company cars with a CO_2 emissions level of more than 75g/km, but no more than 120g/km, is just 10% of the original list price of the car when new.

The 'rounding down' described above does not apply in this case, but the usual 3% supplement does apply to diesel cars.

For a five year period from 6th April 2010 to 5th April 2015, the annual benefit in kind charge on cars with CO_2 emissions of no more than 75g/km will be just 5%.

Alternative Fuels

Prior to 2011/12, discounts applied to reduce the benefit in kind charge on cars which ran on alternative or 'environmentally friendly' fuels. Sadly, these discounts were abolished with effect from 6th April 2011.

Vans

Vans (including so-called 'double cab pick-ups') used privately by employees are subject to a fixed benefit in kind charge of £3,000. An additional charge of £550 applies where private fuel is also provided.

With a maximum cost of £1,420 for a typical higher rate taxpayer, vans must be regarded as 'a bit of a bargain' compared to company cars!

Furthermore, unlike a car, pure home to work travel (with no detours) in a van is not regarded as private use for benefit in kind purposes.

Zero Emission Cars and Vans

Cars and vans which cannot produce any CO_2 emissions under any circumstances (e.g. electric vehicles) are exempt from any benefit in kind charge for a period of five years commencing 6th April 2010.

Fuel Benefit

The chargeable benefit in kind for the provision of private fuel to employees with company cars has been increased drastically over the last few years as a matter of deliberate Government policy. We have also been warned that further increases 'at least in line with the Retail Prices Index' will be made in the future.

The fuel benefit, like the car benefit itself, is based on the car's CO_2 emissions level.

The same percentage which applies for the purposes of the car benefit is multiplied by a set figure, currently £18,800, to produce the amount of the chargeable benefit in kind.

For 2011/12 the chargeable benefit in kind for private fuel may be as much as £6,580, giving rise to combined Income Tax and Class 1A National Insurance costs of up to £3,540 for a typical higher rate taxpayer and even as much as £4,856 in some cases.

Recent increases in fuel prices mean that these tax costs do not look as bad as they once did. Nevertheless, the cost of this benefit is still high enough to mean that some employees would be better off if they simply relinquished it, *even with no compensation from their employers!*

For employers, this situation provides tremendous scope for tax and cost savings and this lends further weight to the wisdom of reviewing the whole company car scheme.

The fuel benefit charge applies in full regardless of how much private travel is paid for by the employer.

It is, however, proportionately reduced if the employee ceases to receive free fuel from their employer part way through the tax year (and does not receive it again that year).

Furthermore, where the employee is required to reimburse all private mileage fuel costs to their employer before, or very shortly after, the end of the tax year, this excessively draconian benefit in kind charge may be avoided altogether.

An employee using a company car for business travel but paying for their fuel privately may claim a tax-free mileage allowance from their employer. The mileage rates in this case are somewhat lower, as it is only intended to reimburse the fuel cost, rather than the car's total running costs.

The current mileage rates (effective from 1st March 2011) applying to the reimbursement of fuel costs incurred by an employee driving a company car on business are as follows:

Engine size	Petrol Cars	Diesel Cars
1,400cc or less	14p	13p
1,401cc to 2,000cc	16p	13p
Over 2,000cc	23p	16p

These rates are reviewed at least twice each year: on 1st June and 1st December, but may also be revised at more frequent intervals when fuel prices have fluctuated significantly since the previous review.

The current rates can be found at:
www.hmrc.gov.uk/cars/advisory_fuel_current.htm

Previous rates can be found at:
www.hmrc.gov.uk/cars/advisory_fuel_archive.htm

Example

Sanjeev's company car is subject to a benefit in kind charge of 35%. He is also provided with fuel by his employer which, for 2011/12, will give rise to a benefit in kind charge of £6,580 costing Sanjeev £2,632 in

Income Tax and costing his employer £908 in Class 1A National Insurance Contributions.

Sanjeev drives 10,000 miles per year on company business but only around 4,000 private miles, even including his short home to work journey.

The total cost of the fuel used by Sanjeev in 2011/12 is £3,000. He calculates that, had he purchased all of his fuel personally, he could claim back £2,300 from his employer in respect of his business mileage, made up as follows:

10,000 miles at 23p/mile =   £2,300

Sanjeev therefore reimburses the net sum of £700 to his employer (£3,000 less £2,300) and thus avoids an Income Tax charge of £2,632. Overall, this leaves him £1,932 better off!

Sanjeev's employer will also save a total of £1,608 (£908 plus the £700 reimbursed by Sanjeev). The combined savings therefore total £3,540 and everyone (except HM Revenue and Customs) is happy.

Not everyone's position will work out as well as Sanjeev's, but it's got to be worth doing the sums!

Note that this only works if the employee is required to reimburse the fuel cost, and actually does so. Since both the employer and the employee benefit, this will generally be acceptable to both parties.

Multiple Tax Increases

On 6th April 2011, the multiplier used to calculate the benefit in kind on the provision of private fuel for use by an employee driving a company car was increased from £18,000 to £18,800.

In most cases, this will combine with the reduction in the CO_2 emissions thresholds to produce a double increase. For example, for a petrol car with CO_2 emissions of 162g/km, the fuel benefit would have been £3,780 (£18,000 x 21%) in 2010/11, but will now be £4,136 (£18,800 x 22%).

Furthermore, the rate of Class 1A National Insurance payable by the employer has also increased from 12.8% to 13.8%. The amount of National Insurance payable by the employer on this benefit will therefore have increased from £484 (£3,780 x 12.8%) in 2010/11 to £571 (£4,136 x 13.8%) in 2011/12: an overall increase of 18%!

Cars Not Available

Both car and fuel benefits are proportionately reduced if a company car is not available to an employee, or is incapable of being used, for a period of at least 30 days during the tax year.

To make a car 'not available', it is generally necessary to ensure that the keys are handed over and retained by the company.

This may be worth considering as a means of reducing these benefits if, for example, an employee is ill or is abroad on holiday for a long period.

Chapter 11

How to Increase Your Tax Credits

Child Tax Credits and Working Tax Credits are completely misnamed as they are not given through the Income Tax self-assessment system and must be claimed directly from HM Revenue & Customs.

Although their names include the word 'tax' (and they are also administered by HM Revenue & Customs), these are not true tax credits at all and are really benefits in another guise.

Nevertheless, working families with combined annual household income of *over £90,000* may sometimes be due some tax credits!

In fact, there is no theoretical limit to the income level at which you may still be eligible for tax credits: if you have enough children.

Even a couple with no children may be able to claim credits of up to £4,660.

Tax Credit Claims

The important thing to note is that Tax Credit claims cannot be backdated by more than three months (and this may be reduced to just one month from 2012/13 onwards under current Government proposals).

Hence, anyone who is (or may be) entitled to claim credits for any tax year must get their claims in to HM Revenue & Customs by 5th July within that tax year in order to obtain their full entitlement (or by 5th May from 2012/13 onwards).

Even if you've missed this deadline, it is worth getting your claim in as soon as possible.

Provisional Claims

Even if you do not think that you are likely to be entitled to any credits, it may be worth submitting a provisional claim.

Although your original tax credit assessment may work out at nil because your income is too high, a provisional claim made by 5th July (or 5th May from 2012/13 onwards) will preserve your full year's entitlement.

A provisional claim made later in the tax year may still preserve a significant proportion of your entitlement for that year. For example, a claim made on 5th February 2012 could be backdated to 5th November 2011 and would therefore enable you to obtain 5/12ths of your entitlement for 2011/12.

A provisional claim may later prove to be highly beneficial. There are many reasons why this may be the case, including:

- An unexpected dip in your level of taxable income
- Redundancy
- Long-term illness
- Domestic problems – breaking up with your spouse or partner, etc
- Death of spouse or partner
- A large capital allowances claim

In short, none of us can be certain what may transpire between now and the end of the tax year.

Hence, to maximise any tax credits that you may later become entitled to, it is worth making backdated provisional claims by 5th July, or 5th May from 2012 onwards, (or as soon as possible thereafter) in almost every case!

Chapter 12

How to Pay Less Capital Gains Tax

The New Capital Gains Tax Regime

For capital gains arising after 22nd June 2010, individuals pay Capital Gains Tax at three rates:

- 10% where entrepreneurs' relief is available (see below)
- 18% on other gains made by basic rate taxpayers
- 28% on other gains made by higher rate taxpayers

The higher rate of 28% applies to capital gains made by an individual during 2011/12 to the extent that:

i) Their total taxable income for 2011/12 (after deducting their personal allowance and any other available deductions), plus

ii) Their total taxable capital gains for the year,

exceeds the Income Tax basic rate band of £35,000.

Individuals who have sufficient income in 2011/12 to fully utilise their basic rate band will therefore pay Capital Gains Tax at 28% on all gains arising during the year (except where entrepreneurs' relief is available).

Basic rate taxpayer individuals will pay Capital Gains Tax at 18% on the first part of any gains arising in the year until their basic rate band is exhausted. Thereafter, any further gains made in the year will be taxed at 28%. (All subject to any entrepreneurs' relief which may be available.)

The 'Explanatory Example' below explains how this works in practice.

Trusts and estates of deceased persons now pay Capital Gains Tax at 28% on all capital gains.

Utilising the Annual Capital Gains Tax Exemption

The annual exemption stands at £10,600 for 2011/12. Capital gains of up to the amount of the annual exemption may be realised tax-free each tax year.

Where possible, taxpayers should consider making use of this exemption before the end of the tax year on 5th April 2012. Once this date passes, this year's exemption is lost completely. It's a case of 'Use It or Lose It'.

Explanatory Example

Indira is a property investor with several 'buy-to-let' investments. In December 2011, she sells a property and realises a capital gain of £40,000.

Indira's taxable income for 2011/12 is £35,475 meaning that £7,000 of her basic rate band remains available (£42,475 - £35,475).

Indira deducts her annual exemption of £10,600 from the £40,000 gain, leaving a taxable gain of £29,400. The first £7,000 is taxed at 18% and the remainder at 28%, giving her a Capital Gains Tax bill on this gain of:

£7,000 x 18% = *£1,260*
£22,400 x 28% = *£6,272*
Total *£7,532*

Indira is therefore due to pay Capital Gains Tax of £7,532 on 31st January 2013 (there are no instalment payments for Capital Gains Tax).

Further Annual Exemption Benefits

Both members of a married couple or civil partnership have their own annual exemption, as do minor children.

The estate of a deceased person has its own annual exemption in the tax year of the death and the following two tax years.

Trusts also have their own annual exemption equal to half of the annual exemption available to individuals (i.e. £5,300 for 2011/12). However, this amount must be sub-divided amongst all of the trusts set up by the same settlor (but with a minimum annual exemption level of £530).

Bed and Breakfasting

The old practice known as 'Bed and Breakfasting' is no longer possible in its simplest form (selling assets, usually quoted shares, and buying them back the next day in order to utilise the annual exemption).

There are, however, still a number of ways in which a similar approach can be used in order to utilise the annual exemption:

i) Wait 31 days before buying the shares back. (This is fine for Capital Gains Tax planning purposes, but does not always appeal to those who wish to stay in the market.)

ii) 'Bed and Spousing' – for a couple (married or not), there is a very simple mechanism available. One partner sells the shares and the other one makes an equivalent purchase. (For married couples and civil partners the repurchase must be made on the open market – a direct sale from one spouse or partner to the other will not have the desired effect.)

iii) 'Bed and ISA' – sell the shares in order to realise your annual exemption and buy them back (again on the open market) through an ISA. It is, however, unlikely that you will be able to utilise the whole annual exemption in this way.

iv) 'Bed and Trust' – sell the shares and buy them back on the open market through a trust.

v) 'Bed and Company' – sell the shares and buy them back on the open market through a company.

If following (iv) or (v) above, note that different tax regimes apply to trusts and companies. Furthermore, trusts created during the settlor's lifetime may be subject to Inheritance Tax charges (see the Taxcafe.co.uk guide *'How to Avoid Inheritance Tax'* for further details).

Method (ii) works just as well where the repurchase is carried out by another family member. It is even possible to make the repurchase in the name of a minor child; although the shares would then need to be held on 'bare trust' and this has other tax consequences for the parent.

Utilising Capital Losses

Capital losses are, in the first instance, automatically set off against capital gains arising in the same tax year. Any surplus is carried forward for set off against future gains (but only to the extent that the future gains exceed the annual exemption). Generally speaking, capital losses may not be carried back to earlier tax years.

This has a couple of important practical implications:

- Losses must be realised by 5th April 2012 in order to be set off against 2011/12 capital gains.

- If the losses realised during any tax year reduce the net capital gains for that tax year below the level of the annual exemption, some of this exemption is effectively lost.

Hence, the timing of the disposal of assets standing at a loss should be considered carefully, bearing the above points in mind.

HM Revenue and Customs has the power to deny relief for capital losses where they perceive that the loss arose as a result of transactions which were carried out with a main purpose of creating a tax advantage. They state, however, that they will not use this power in the case of 'normal prudent tax planning'. Time will tell how this phrase is actually interpreted in practice.

Entrepreneurs' Relief

Entrepreneurs' relief applies in certain limited circumstances: generally on the sale of a trading business, qualifying furnished holiday letting property, or shares in qualifying companies.

The total capital gains made by any individual on which the relief may be claimed is subject to a lifetime limit, as follows:

- Gains arising between 6th April 2008 and 5th April 2010: £1m
- Gains arising between 6th April and 22nd June 2010: £2m
- Gains arising between 23rd June 2010 and 5th April 2011: £5m
- Gains arising on or after 6th April 2011: £10m

For example, an individual who made qualifying gains of £1.2m in 2009, £1.4m in May 2010, £4m in July 2010 and £7m in January 2012 could claim entrepreneurs' relief on:

- £1m of the gain in 2009 (the lifetime limit then applying),
- £1m of the gain in May 2010 (the limit of £2m then applying less the £1m already claimed),
- £3m of the gain in July 2010 (the limit of £5m then applying less the £2m already claimed), and
- £5m of the gain in 2012 (the new limit of £10m less the £5m already claimed).

For qualifying gains arising after 22nd June 2010, a simple 10% rate is applied. Such gains must be counted for the purposes of determining whether the taxpayer's basic rate band has been fully utilised and must be taken in priority to other gains.

Generally speaking, however, the taxpayer may allocate their annual exemption and any available capital losses to any other capital gains arising in the same tax year in preference to gains eligible for entrepreneurs' relief.

Enterprise Investment Scheme (EIS) Shares

Capital Gains Tax may be deferred by reinvesting gains in EIS shares. The investment must take place within the four-year period which begins a year before the date of the disposal that gave rise to the gain and which ends three years after that date.

Although the annual limit of £500,000 (increasing to £1m from 2012/13 under current Government proposals) only applies to Income Tax relief on EIS shares (see Chapter 3), in the case of very large gains it may be worth making this maximum investment in each relevant tax year, to maximise the combined Income Tax and Capital Gains Tax relief.

Example

Jerry anticipates making a taxable gain of £5 million in May 2012. He could defer all of the Capital Gains Tax arising on this gain by reinvesting it in Enterprise Investment Scheme shares, as follows:

- *£1m between June 2011 and 5ᵗʰ April 2012 (of which, £500,000 can be carried back for Income Tax relief in 2010/11 – see Chapter 3)*
- *£1m during the 2012/13 tax year*
- *£1m during the 2013/14 tax year*
- *£1m during the 2014/15 tax year*
- *£1m between 6ᵗʰ April 2015 and the third anniversary of his original capital gain*

In this way, not only would Jerry defer his entire Capital Gains Tax liability, but he would also have made total Income Tax savings of up to £1,450,000. His total tax saving/deferral could thus be up to £2,850,000!

The great drawback to EIS investments has, of course, always been the fact that they are inherently risky by nature.

However, there are now some Enterprise Investment Scheme-based investments available which are structured on a portfolio system, thus spreading the risk considerably. Whilst this doesn't remove all of the risk from these types of investment, it certainly improves the odds! See your IFA for further details.

Emigration

Some years ago, it was possible, under certain circumstances, to be treated as non-UK resident for Capital Gains Tax purposes immediately on departure from the UK. Sadly, this facility is no longer available and a taxpayer generally remains liable to UK Capital Gains Tax on any gains arising during the tax year in which they emigrate.

Hence, if intending to avoid UK Capital Gains Tax on a gain due to arise in 2012/13 by emigrating abroad, you should ensure that you leave the UK by 5th April 2012 at the latest.

Furthermore, to avoid a clawback of Capital Gains Tax on your return, you will need to remain non-UK resident for at least five complete UK tax years. Those emigrating during 2011/12 to avoid UK Capital Gains Tax need to plan on staying away until at least 6th April 2017.

Non-residence can sometimes be maintained despite some limited return visits to the UK, not exceeding:

- 182 days in any one UK tax year, and
- 90 days per UK tax year on average.

From 6th April 2008, any day on which you are present in the UK at midnight is counted for the purpose of these tests unless you are merely in transit from one foreign country to another.

It is important to understand, however, that the tests given above are intended as basic guidelines only. These basic rules are just the beginning. They are effectively just a preliminary test which a taxpayer must pass before we can even begin to consider if they might be non-UK resident.

Recent case law suggests that a much harsher view is now being taken on the question of emigration. In practice, it is not sufficient just to meet the basic rules set out above and the taxpayer's overall situation must be reviewed to determine if they can genuinely be regarded as non-UK resident.

The position may become a little clearer in future, as the Government is hoping to introduce a statutory residence test from April 2012, following a period of consultation.

Reporting Capital Gains

You will need to report capital gains arising during the year on your tax return if:

i)   You have any Capital Gains Tax liability, or
ii)   Your total sale proceeds for capital disposals made during the year exceed four times the annual exemption (i.e. £42,400 for disposals during 2011/12).

The proceeds of any property disposals which are wholly covered by the principal private residence exemption (e.g. the sale of your own main residence) may be excluded for the purposes of test (ii) above. See the Taxcafe.co.uk guide *'How to Avoid Property Tax'* for a detailed explanation of the application of this exemption.

It is also important to report capital disposals which give rise to an overall capital loss for the tax year, so that you can claim to carry this loss forward to future years.

If you are not already in the self-assessment system and need to report a capital gain or loss, it is important to advise HM Revenue and Customs as soon as possible after the end of the relevant tax year (for the same reasons that we considered in Chapter 5 in respect of new sources of untaxed income).

Chapter 13

How to Pay Less Inheritance Tax

Prior to dissolving Parliament for the General Election in May 2010, the old Labour Government announced that it intended to freeze the Inheritance Tax nil rate band for five years.

Sadly, despite previous Conservative promises to increase the nil rate band to £1m, the new Coalition Government has also adopted this Labour policy.

It therefore appears that the Inheritance Tax nil rate band is likely to remain at its current level of £325,000 until at least 5th April 2015.

A modest average rate of annual inflation of, say, 3.5% would reduce the value of this exemption in real terms to just £273,000 by the end of this period, making Inheritance Tax planning as important as it has ever been.

Generally speaking, effective Inheritance Tax planning should be carried out on a long-term basis. However, it is worth remembering the following points, which should be considered on an annual basis.

Annual Exemption

The first £3,000 of gifts made by any individual in each tax year is totally exempt from Inheritance Tax.

Furthermore, if last year's annual exemption has not been fully utilised, it may still be used to exempt gifts in excess of £3,000. Hence, if an individual has not made any gifts during this or the previous tax year, the first £6,000 of gifts made between now and the end of the tax year will be fully exempt.

As with Capital Gains Tax, each partner in a married couple or civil partnership has their own annual exemption.

Small Gifts Exemption

Gifts of up to £250 per tax year made to any one individual are also exempt from Inheritance Tax and do not count towards the annual exemption.

The donor may make as many such gifts as he or she wishes (all to different recipients). The annual exemption may not, however, be used for further gifts to the same recipient in the same tax year.

Example

Donald has three sons: Huey, Dewey and Louis. He makes the best use of his annual and small gifts exemptions by making three gifts every year – a gift of £3,000 to one son and gifts of £250 to each of his other two sons. To make it fair, he simply changes which son gets the larger gift each year and, over every three-year period, they all receive the same.

Habitual Gifts Out Of Income

There is a general exemption from Inheritance Tax for habitual gifts out of income. In order for such gifts to be 'habitual', they should generally be made regularly for a number of years. Hence, it is important to remember to make any such gifts again this year.

Chapter 14

Tax Tips for Non-Domiciled Individuals

A UK resident but non-UK domiciled individual is entitled to claim exemption from UK Income Tax and Capital Gains Tax on income or capital gains arising abroad unless and until such time as the relevant income or sales proceeds are remitted to the UK.

This is known as the 'remittance basis' and is also available to a person who is UK resident but not ordinarily resident in the UK.

Unfortunately, however, the remittance basis now comes at a heavy price.

Any UK resident claiming the remittance basis who has unremitted overseas income and capital gains of £2,000 or more in the tax year will lose their personal allowance and their Capital Gains Tax annual exemption.

Worse still, any adult claiming the remittance basis who has been UK resident for at least seven of the previous nine tax years, is also subject to an additional annual charge of £30,000. This charge does not apply, however, where an individual has less than £2,000 of unremitted overseas income and capital gains for the year.

Those subject to the £30,000 charge will also be subject to Capital Gains Tax at 28% on all capital gains, regardless of the level of their income (unless they are able to claim entrepreneurs' relief – see Chapter 12).

Opting Out

Each individual may 'opt out' of the remittance basis on a year by year basis in order to avoid the £30,000 charge and retain the benefit of the Income Tax personal allowance and the Capital Gains Tax annual exemption.

Opting out applies for one year only and does not affect the individual's underlying non-UK domiciled or non-ordinarily resident status. This means that for the next year, or any subsequent year, they may claim the remittance basis once again if this becomes more beneficial.

This introduces a significant amount of choice for non-UK domiciled or non-ordinarily resident individuals resident in the UK and gives rise to some useful tax planning strategies.

The question of 'in or out', i.e. whether to opt out of the remittance basis, needs to be considered differently at various different levels of overseas income and capital gains.

The matter is further complicated by the fact that each individual can only make one overall decision, for each tax year, whether to claim the remittance basis on both their overseas income and their overseas capital gains. In practice, many people will have a mixture of both income and capital gains and will need to work out the best course of action under their own particular circumstances.

Furthermore, the position is also dependent on the level of taxable UK income or capital gains which the individual already has.

What follows is therefore merely a set of rough guidelines to consider when deciding whether to opt out of the remittance basis for 2011/12.

It is important to note that the guidelines set out below relate to the individual's UK tax position only and are therefore subject to the impact of any double tax relief which may be available.

Overseas Income under £2,000

Where the overseas income and capital gains for the year totals less than £2,000, the remittance basis can be claimed without incurring any extra tax charges in the UK. This enables a non-UK domiciled or non-ordinarily resident individual to accumulate up to £1,999 a year in tax-free overseas income.

Overseas Income between £2,000 and £9,474

Where the total overseas income and capital gains for the year lies in this bracket, the same saving can be preserved by remitting all but £1,999 of the overseas income and gains back to the UK during the tax year.

Gains should generally be remitted in preference to income since these will either be covered by the annual exemption or be taxed at a lower rate.

In fact, capital gains of up to the amount of the annual exemption could often effectively be remitted back to the UK tax free if this reduces the total unremitted overseas income and gains for the year to less than £2,000.

All of the above is technically still possible where the £30,000 charge is applicable, but unless you're absolutely certain of your figures, I wouldn't tend to risk it and would suggest opting out of the remittance basis instead.

Those with existing taxable income of £114,950 or more are already in the same position as under the next income bracket described below, as they will already have lost their personal allowance in any case.

Overseas Income between £9,475 and £60,000

Where a non-UK domiciled or non-ordinarily resident individual has unremitted overseas income of over £9,475, but is not subject to the £30,000 charge, it will generally be worth claiming the remittance basis since the tax saved will more than compensate for the loss of the personal allowance.

The loss of the Capital Gains Tax annual exemption must also be taken into account, however, as this may create additional liabilities of up to £2,968 (£10,600 @ 28%) on any capital gains on UK assets in the same year.

Where the £30,000 charge does apply, it will not usually be worth claiming the remittance basis where the unremitted overseas income does not exceed £60,000 (subject to any potential Capital Gains Tax liabilities on unremitted overseas gains).

Overseas Income between £60,000 and £105,356

Where the individual is not subject to the £30,000 charge, they will definitely benefit from claiming the remittance basis.

Where the £30,000 charge does apply, the position will depend on the level of UK income and capital gains which the person has.

Overseas Income over £105,356

Once the overseas income reaches this level, the remittance basis will be preferable in all cases.

Capital Gains

The position on overseas capital gains is slightly different, as these are subject to different tax rates to income when taxable in the UK (see Chapter 12).

As indicated above, overseas capital gains of up to the amount of the annual exemption may be remitted back to the UK tax free where the individual has no UK capital gains in the same tax year and has other overseas income and gains of less than £2,000.

Where an individual has overseas capital gains slightly above the amount of the annual exemption, it may be preferable to either remit them back to the UK or to opt out of the remittance basis in order to preserve the individual's personal allowance (unless the individual already has taxable income of £114,950 or more).

However, an individual who is not subject to the £30,000 charge and has total overseas capital gains in excess of £23,278 will generally be better off claiming the remittance basis.

For those who are subject to the £30,000 charge, a much larger overseas capital gain will generally be required before it is beneficial to claim the remittance basis, although this does depend on the level of unremitted overseas income which also arises in the same UK tax year and the level of the individual's existing taxable income and UK capital gains in that year.

Nevertheless, where an individual has an unremitted overseas capital gain in excess of £137,582, the remittance basis will generally be worth claiming.

Saving or Deferral?

It is worth remembering that the remittance basis may sometimes only defer UK tax on foreign income and gains. If the funds are brought into the UK at a later date whilst the investor is still UK resident then tax may arise at that time. Hence, it will generally only be worth claiming the remittance basis if:

i)   The overseas income and gains are to remain offshore permanently,

ii)   The investor will cease to be UK resident before the funds are remitted, or

iii) The funds can be remitted to the UK at a future date with the benefit of an exemption from UK tax (see 'Changes Ahead' below).

Planning for Non-Domiciles

Non-UK domiciled and non-ordinarily resident individuals can reduce the impact of the charges levied for claiming the remittance basis in a number of ways.

The £30,000 charge can be avoided by ensuring that you are non-UK resident for three years out of every ten.

Those who are in their seventh year of UK residence might wish to consider realising capital gains on all of their overseas assets now before the £30,000 charge comes into force.

Capital gains on overseas assets can be 'realised' by selling the asset to an unconnected third party or by transferring it to a trust, a company or another individual such as an unmarried partner or adult child (but not to your spouse or civil partner). The capital gain arising at this stage will escape UK tax by claiming the remittance basis and any subsequent taxable gain will be limited to the asset's future growth in value.

Wealth Warning

When realising capital gains on overseas assets for UK tax planning purposes, it is essential to take any potential foreign tax liabilities into account.

If the £30,000 charge already applies to you, it may be beneficial to ensure that all, or several, of your capital gains on foreign assets fall into the same UK tax year. In this way, UK Capital Gains Tax can be avoided on all of your disposals for the price of one £30,000 charge rather than several.

Example

Kyrano is non-UK domiciled but has been resident in the UK for ten years. He owns two properties in the Pacific territory of the Hood Islands where there is no tax on capital gains. Kyrano also has a large portfolio of investments in the UK and always uses his Capital Gains Tax annual exemption and basic rate Income Tax band.

In December 2011, Kyrano sells one of his Hood Islands properties and makes a capital gain of £200,000. As this will give rise to UK Capital Gains Tax of £56,000 (at 28%), it will be worth Kyrano claiming the remittance basis for 2011/12 and paying the £30,000 charge.

Kyrano is also anticipating selling his other Hood Islands property shortly and expects that it will also yield a capital gain of around £200,000. If he sells his second property by 5th April 2012, he can avoid UK Capital Gains Tax on this sale without incurring any further UK tax charges.

If, on the other hand, Kyrano sells his second overseas property on or after 6th April 2012, he will have to pay a further £30,000 charge in order to avoid UK Capital Gains Tax (plus bear the cost of losing his personal allowance and Capital Gains Tax annual exemption for 2012/13).

If Kyrano cannot, or would prefer not to, sell his second Hood Islands property by 5th April 2012, he might wish to consider 'realising' a capital gain on the property using one of the methods described above.

Couples

Where a couple are both UK resident but either non-UK domiciled or non-ordinarily resident in the UK, it may make sense to transfer all or most of their overseas assets to one of them. UK tax can then be avoided on unremitted overseas income and capital gains for the price of just one lost personal allowance, Capital Gains Tax annual exemption and £30,000 charge where applicable.

In some cases, it may also make sense for the couple's overseas assets to be transferred to the one who has been UK resident for fewer years (i.e. where one or both of them have been UK resident for less than seven of the previous nine years). This will delay the impact of the £30,000 charge for as long as possible.

Changes Ahead

The Government is proposing to make two important changes to the taxation of individuals claiming the remittance basis from 2012/13 onwards.

Firstly, they propose to exempt funds remitted for commercial investments in the UK from taxation under the remittance basis.

Secondly, they propose to levy an annual charge of £50,000 (instead of £30,000) on non-domiciled taxpayers claiming the remittance basis who have been UK resident for 12 or more years.

These proposals give rise to some important tax planning considerations for UK resident individuals entitled to claim the remittance basis, including:

- Anyone planning to remit funds for the purposes of commercial investments in the UK may wish to consider delaying their remittance until at least 6th April 2012.

- Those who have currently been UK resident for 11 or more years may wish to consider realising overseas capital gains during 2011/12 using some of the methods described above. In this way, UK Capital Gains Tax can be avoided at a cost of £30,000, rather than £50,000.

114

- Couples where one or both of the individuals have currently been UK resident for less than 11 years may wish to consider transferring overseas assets to the one who has been UK resident for fewer years.

Chapter 15

Some Final Tax Tips

State Pension Entitlement

Earlier in this guide, I mentioned that certain types of income are exempt from National Insurance of any class.

The only drawback to a complete exemption from National Insurance is the fact that this may adversely affect your state pension entitlement.

For employees (including company directors) full state pension entitlement can usually be maintained at no tax cost by paying a salary of between £5,459 and £7,075.

Self-employed taxpayers may choose to continue paying Class 2 National Insurance at £2.50 per week in order to maintain their entitlement, even when profits fall under the small earnings exception of £5,315.

Other taxpayers concerned about their state pension entitlement may wish to consider paying voluntary Class 3 National Insurance.

The rate of Class 3 contributions has, however, increased dramatically in recent years and now stands at £12.60 per week. At an annual cost of £655.20, this is by far the most expensive option and the other methods outlined above are therefore to be preferred, where available.

Civil Partnerships

Since December 2005, same-sex couples entering into registered civil partnerships have been treated exactly the same as legally married couples for all UK tax purposes. This has both advantages and disadvantages, just as it always has done for married couples. More details are available in the Taxcafe.co.uk guide *'How Couples Save Tax'*.

Appendix A

UK Tax Rates and Allowances: 2010/11 to 2012/13

	Rates	2010/11 £	2011/12 £	2012/13 £
Income Tax				
Personal allowance		6,475	7,475	8,105
Basic rate band	20%	37,400	35,000	34,370
Higher rate/Threshold	40%	43,875	42,475	42,475
Personal allowance withdrawal				
Effective rate/From	60%	100,000	100,000	100,000
To		112,950	114,950	116,210
Super tax rate/Threshold	50%	150,000	150,000	150,000

Starting rate band applying to interest and other savings income only

	Rates	2010/11	2011/12	2012/13
	10%	2,440	2,560	2,710*
National Insurance				
Class 1 – Primary		11%	12%	12%
Class 4		8%	9%	9%
Primary threshold		5,715	7,225	7,555*
Upper earnings limit		43,875	42,475	42,475
Additional Rate		1%	2%	2%
Class 1 – Secondary		12.8%	13.8%	13.8%
Secondary threshold		5,715	7,075	7,475*
Class 2 – per week		2.40	2.50	2.65*
Small earnings exception		5,075	5,315	5,555*
Class 3 – per week		12.05	12.60	13.20*
Pension Contributions				
Annual allowance		255,000	50,000	50,000
Lifetime allowance		1.8m	1.8m	1.5m
Capital Gains Tax				
Annual exemption		10,100	10,600	11,100*
Basic rate		18%	18%	18%
Higher rate		28% (1)	28%	28%
Entrepreneurs' relief:				
Lifetime limit		2m/5m (1)	10m	10m
Rate of relief/Tax rate		4/9ths/10%(1)	10%	10%
Inheritance Tax				
Nil Rate Band		325,000	325,000	325,000
Annual Exemption		3,000	3,000	3,000

Age-related Allowances, etc.

Age allowance: 65-74	9,490	9,940	10,500*
Age allowance: 75 and over	9,640	10,090	10,660*
MCA: born before 6/4/1935 (2)	6,965	7,295	7,705*
MCA minimum	2,670	2,800	2,960*
Income limit	22,900	24,000	25,400*
Blind Person's Allowance	1,890	1,980	2,100*

* - Estimated, based on inflation at 5.6% (per RPI) and 4.5% (per CPI).

Notes
1. Capital Gains Tax changes were introduced with effect from 23 June 2010.
2. The Married Couples Allowance, 'MCA', is given at a rate of 10%.

Appendix B

Forecast Future Tax Rates and Allowances

	Rates	Bands, allowances, etc.		
		2013/14 £	2014/15 £	2015/16 £
Income Tax				
Personal allowance		8,735	9,365	10,000
Basic rate band	20%	33,740	34,235	34,700
Higher rate threshold	40%	42,475	43,600	44,700
Personal allowance withdrawal				
Effective rate/ From	60%	100,000	100,000	100,000
To		117,470	118,730	120,000
Super tax rate threshold	50%	150,000	150,000	150,000
Starting rate band applying to savings income only				
	10%	2,810	2,910	3,020
Capital Gains Tax				
Annual exemption		11,400	11,700	12,000
Inheritance Tax				
Nil Rate Band		325,000	325,000	334,000
Age-related Allowances				
Age allowance: 65 -74		10,870	11,260	11,660
Age allowance: 75 & over		11,040	11,430	11,840
MCA maximum		7,975	8,255	8,545
MCA minimum		3,070	3,180	3,300
Income limit		26,300	27,300	28,300
National Insurance				
Class 1 Rate		12%	12%	12%
Class 4 Rate		9%	9%	9%
Additional Rate		2%	2%	2%
Primary Threshold		7,745	7,945	8,145
Secondary Threshold		7,745	8,025	8,315
Upper Earnings Limit		42,475	43,600	44,700
Class 2 per week		£2.75	£2.85	£2.95

Disclaimer

1. Please note that this tax guide is intended as general guidance only for individual readers and does NOT constitute accountancy, tax, investment or other professional advice. Neither Taxcafe UK Limited nor the author can accept any responsibility or liability for loss which may arise from reliance on information contained in this tax guide.

2. Please note that tax legislation, the law and practices by government and regulatory authorities (e.g. HM Revenue & Customs) are constantly changing. We therefore recommend that for accountancy, tax, investment or other professional advice, you consult a suitably qualified accountant, tax specialist, independent financial adviser, or other professional adviser. Please also note that your personal circumstances may vary from the general examples given in this tax guide and your professional adviser will be able to give specific advice based on your personal circumstances.

3. This tax guide covers UK taxation only and any references to 'tax' or 'taxation' in this tax guide, unless the contrary is expressly stated, are to UK taxation only. Please note that references to the 'UK' do not include the Channel Islands or the Isle of Man. Addressing all foreign tax implications is beyond the scope of this tax guide.

4. Whilst in an effort to be helpful, this tax guide may refer to general guidance on matters other than UK taxation, Taxcafe UK Limited and the author are not experts in these matters and do not accept any responsibility or liability for loss which may arise from reliance on such information contained in this tax guide.

5. Please note that Taxcafe UK Limited has relied wholly upon the expertise of the author in the preparation of the content of this tax guide. The author is not an employee of Taxcafe UK Limited but has been selected by Taxcafe UK Limited using reasonable care and skill to write the content of this tax guide.

Lightning Source UK Ltd.
Milton Keynes UK
UKOW021332270911

179385UK00001B/9/P